Ooka Makoto is the author of 18 collections of poetry and more than 150 volumes of essays on literature and the arts.

Although perhaps better known for his modern poetry, Ooka Makoto is a distinguished waka poet. He is also a major critic of poetry, perhaps the finest in Japan today.

Donald Keene

Through the richness of Ooka's work we find once again the abundance of our spiritual and natural heritage.

Tanikawa Shuntaro

Mr. Ooka has received the Ministry of Education Award, and the *Gendaishi, Hanatsubaki, Kikuchi Kan, Mugen, Rekitei* and *Yomiuri* prizes. He is President of PEN, Japan.

Japanese names are given in the traditional order, family name first.

Also from Katydid Books by Mr. Ooka --

A String Around Autumn, poems
Elegy and Benediction, poems
A Play of Mirrors: *Eight Major Poets of Modern Japan*, anthology

The Colors of Poetry

Series

REFLECTIONS

Editor

Thomas Fitzsimmons

The Colors of Poetry
Essays in Classic Japanese Verse

Ooka Makoto

Translated by

Takako U. Lento
Thomas V. Lento

Preface by Donald Keene

Katydid Books
Oakland University

Michigan

Produced by KT DID Productions, Inc
Printed in the United States of America
by Thomson-Shore, Dexter, MI

This book is printed on acid-free paper and its binding materials have been chosen for strength and durability.

KATYDID BOOKS:
K.H.-Fitzsimmons and T. Fitzsimmons, assisted by G.L. Robinson
c/o Department of English, Oakland University, Rochester, MI 48309-4401
FAX 313-370-2286

This book is published with the aid of a grant from the Saison Cultural Foundation (Japan).

Library of Congress Cataloging in Publication Data

Ooka, Makoto, 1931-
    The colors of poetry : essays on classic Japanese verse / by Ooka
  Makoto ; translated by Takako U. Lento & Thomas V. Lento ; preface
  by Donald Keene.
            p. cm. - - (Reflections)
        Translation from various Japanese books.
        Includes indexes
        ISBN 0-942668-28-6. - - ISBN 0-942668-27-8 (pbk.)
        1. Japanese poetry- -History and criticism.   I. Keene, Donald
  II. Title. III. Series.
  PL727.5.049   1991
  895.6' 1009 - - dc20   91-6796
                                                                  CIP

CONTENTS

Introductory

The Colors of Poetry

Supplementary

Preface

Donald Keene

The only variety of Japanese poetry widely known outside Japan is the *haiku*. Poets in many countries of Europe and America have been so attracted by the brevity of the form and the concentration of its imagery that *haiku* are now composed in various languages. These non-Japanese poets sometimes observe the metrical requirements and the seasonal words, but sometimes they merely set down three lines of "poetic" images and hope for the best. Quite apart from the activities of amateurs, an acquaintance with the *haiku* has enriched the works of major poets, especially those who have taken to heart the prescription of the Japanese *haiku* masters that each word in a poem must be essential and irreplaceable.

The interest displayed in the *haiku* has tended to obscure the existence of a much older poetic form, known in the past as the *waka* but at present more commonly as the *tanka*. The *waka* is the oldest Japanese poetic form: the earliest examples go back to the fifth or sixth century, and there has never been a time since then when *waka* poetry was not composed, whether by courtiers seeking to ingratiate themselves with the women they loved, by soldiers about to be executed, or by quite ordinary people when asked to write something in a guest book. The *waka* is not quite as short as the *haiku* -- 31 syllables as opposed to the 17 syllables of a *haiku* -- but the differences between the two varieties of poetry go far beyond the matter of length. The *haiku* is effective because of its juxtaposition of images, creating surprising contrasts and tensions; the *waka* is generally lyric, conveying directly or indirectly the emotions of the poet.

The functions and ideals of the *waka* have obviously not remained unchanged through the centuries, but have evolved both with the preferences of the times and with the dicta pronounced by the major poets. Poetic criticism devoted to the *waka* goes back to the tenth century, and has developed in parallel to the *waka* itself. Although some of this criticism is technical and not of much interest any longer, the reader is not infrequently startled by comments and judgments that can be applied to the composition of poetry even today. Although longer poetic forms than the *waka* flourished in the seventh and eighth centuries, they gradually disappeared and were not made the subject of criticism in the manner of the *waka*. The loss of the longer forms deprived the poets of the possibility of composing, say, narrative or intellectual poetry that requires more space than 31 syllables, but this did not bother them. What they wished to express in poetry could almost always be encapsulated into a *waka*, and for them it was less important to expand their poetic horizons than to explore the potential of one form, the *waka*, and to communicate one subject, the emotions that spring from seeds in the human heart.

Ooka Makoto, though better known perhaps for his modern poetry (*gendaishi*), is a distinguished *waka* poet. He is also a major critic of poetry, perhaps the finest in Japan today. He writes both as a poet who has returned again and again to the *waka* for its special possibilities of expression, and as a critic who has studied the course of the development of the *waka* over the past millennium. His responses to the poetry contained in the two great anthologies, the *Kokin Waka Shu* of the tenth century and the *Shin Kokin Waka Shu* of the thirteenth century, reveal a scholarly understanding of what the poems meant to readers in their own times and what they mean to ours, and he combines this with the intuitive understanding of the practicing poet of the means the original poets chose to convey their poetic intent.

Mr. Ooka's personal experiences as a poet underlay his discovery of the seemingly contradictory nature of the circumstances under which Japanese poetry has traditionally been composed. Japanese poets, whether in the tenth century or today, tend to belong to groups -- sometimes as disciples of the same great predecessor, sometimes merely as fellow guests at a "banquet," to use Ooka's word. Some varieties of poetry, notably *renga* that flourished especially in the medieval period, require the participation of several poets in the composition of a single chain of linked verse. It often happened too that teams of poets at the court were assigned topics on which to compose competing verses. Linked verse and poetic competitions have lost their appeal, but even today, poets (of whatever variety) tend to cluster together and publish little magazines that assert the claims of a particular group to recognition.

At the same time, poets of all ages have felt the contrary need for solitude. Some have taken refuge in distant hermitages from the poetry-making society of the court, hoping to find new beauty in the external world and new depth in their own souls. But participation in a group or self-imposed isolation was generally not an either/or choice. The great Saigyo is best known for the poetry he composed in solitude, but he also took part from time to time in the activities of the poets at the court. However devoted to solitude a poet may be, if he forsakes totally the companionship of other poets he will be depriving himself of one of the joys of creation, the recognition of his equals.

Mr. Ooka's fresh and penetrating observations on the nature of Japanese poetry tell us much about Japanese civilization as a whole and, ultimately, about the Japanese people. Japanese poetry is distinct in its traditions, sometimes (especially in the love poetry) quite unlike European poetry in its expression, but with Mr. Ooka's guidance it becomes entirely intelligible in terms of what it tells us of emotions and perceptions of universal application.

Introduction

JAPANESE POETRY FROM THE INSIDE

Takako U. Lento
Thomas V. Lento

In *The Colors of Poetry* the reader sees traditional Japanese poetry from the point of view of a Japanese literary person. The author is Ooka Makoto, poet, critic, essayist, and President of the Japan PEN Club.

Ooka presents the poetry of medieval Japan not as an historical curiosity or the arcane study of specialists, but as a living poetic testament whose influence is felt in contemporary life and art. Though based on the latest scholarship, the book's perspective is that of the creative artist.

Ooka's reading first places the poetry within its historical context, then shows its relevance to our own personal, social, and artistic concerns. The key metaphor of the book's "Prologue" is the idea of the complementary "banquet" and "solitary mind." As the leader of one of the most important post-war groups, Ooka gives a first-hand view of the sharing of the creative impulse at a banquet, tea-party, drinking session, or other group activity that is a fixture of Japanese literary world. He also analyzes how the conflict between this communal spirit and the creative struggles of an individual's solitary mind produce the tension inherent in the best poetry from Japan.

The "Epilogue" goes farther. It applies this idea to the present to show how it affects modern poetry, Japanese and non-Japanese. The author offers experiential evidence of its effectiveness in forging new bonds among poets around the world today.

In the body of the book the subject is the classic poetry in its own right. Here Ooka is sympathetic to the way a creative mind must work within its own time. He presents the changing social and political eras, and the shifts in literary and artistic fashions that accompanied them, not as historical artifacts but as contexts for creation. We see poets in times of change staking out new ground from which to express themselves.

Ooka calls on his poet's understanding to let us share the experiences of his subjects. We see inside the minds of these ancient poets and their contemporaries. Each poet comes alive in his or her feelings, sufferings, triumphs. And we explore the subtleties of poetic expression to get a truer understanding of what the poets say in their poems, as well as a better sense of their achievement.

The book also shows how the Japanese language affected and was affected by poetry, and expands the point to illuminate the assumptions, even the thought patterns, of the Japanese. Ooka demonstrates how the word *iro*, or color, came to imply unseemly carnality, and how Japanese-style poetry was restored to officially recognized status when it abandoned *iro*. This offers insight into the understated character of much Japanese art.

He also demonstrates how classical Japanese poetry, when it deals with colors, expresses them indirectly, through the names of objects possessing the colors rather than the names of an organized color spectrum. By showing how Japanese art favors the concrete and sensory to the abstract and intellectualized, he prepares us for the differences between Japanese and Western modes of expression.

MODERN REVERBERATIONS

The "Epilogue" takes us beyond classical times, beyond Japan, into a superheated modern world where people still try to practice poetry. Here Ooka finds the attraction of classical Japanese forms undiminished by time and unfettered by national boundaries.

In 1971 Octavio Paz published *Renga*, a collection of sonnets produced by the collaboration of four poets in the manner of Japanese linked verse. In 1970 Ooka and other poets started their own "banquet" of traditional linked verse (*renku*). One year later Ooka started a cooperative project on linked free verse among the poets associated with his coterie magazine group "*Kai.*"

In 1981 Ooka and Thomas Fitzsimmons published *Rocking Mirror Daybreak*, a book of linked verse they composed in Oakland, Michigan while Ooka was a visiting professor and poet at Oakland University. In the ten years since Ooka has participated in several international "banquets" of linked poems with some of the foremost poets in the world: twice in Germany, where two volumes of their achievements were published in German and in Japanese; once in Helsinki; three times in Rotterdam (a Netherlands literary magazine also published a special issue on linked poems); and once in Paris. In 1990 Ooka and Tanikawa Shuntaro joined two other poets and two translators in Germany to conduct yet another "banquet" of linked verse.

THE GENESIS OF THIS WORK

As a visiting professor and resident poet at Oakland University, Michigan, Ooka Makoto came to realize the need for a book that would give his students a deeper understanding of Japanese literature. He conceived the idea of this book, and proposed to work with the translators to create an English version, re-edited to speak as directly as possible to an English-speaking audience.

It speaks, we believe, as more than a handbook on traditional Japanese poetry. It speaks as a guide to important concepts in Japanese culture.

Translators' Note

Mr. Ooka's purpose in this book, and ours, was to open a window into Japanese poetry for the American reader. This determined the book's translation method as much as it did its content.

The first part of the book, the "Prologue: On Some Characteristics of Japanese Poetic Creation," needed no translation. It is a transcript of an address given by Mr. Ooka in English at a conference at the University of Michigan. He addressed the conference while a visiting poet at Oakland University (Michigan).

The rest of the text is drawn from two different Japanese sources, as selected and edited by Mr. Ooka, with the exception of the "Epilogue: Classic Form, Modern Revival," which he wrote in Japanese especially for this book. In our translation of this material, including all of the poetry cited in it, we have tried not to do a verbatim rendering of the original. Only in this way did we feel we could preserve the spirit of the original.

THE TRANSLATION OF THE PROSE

Chapter one of this book combines material from chapters two and three of Mr. Ooka's *Shi no Nihongo* (*The Language of Japanese Poetry*). Chapters two, three, and four are based respectively on chapters four, eight, and nine of that book, which was published in 1980 by Chuo Koronsha (Tokyo) as Volume XI in their series *Nihongo no Sekai* (The World of the Japanese Language).

These first four chapters are not translations in the strict sense of the word, but rather a re-edited English version of the original. We wanted to reproduce in English the impression of an onrushing flood of ideas that gives the original Japanese its movement. The content is accurate -- Mr. Ooka was involved in the re-editing, as was Professor Thomas Fitzsimmons -- but it has been reshaped to take into account the fact that Americans would be less familiar with the material than would Mr. Ooka's Japanese readers. We hope the result speaks more directly to an American audience.

Chapters five and six of the present work are translations of chapters eight and nine of the 1982 book *Nihon Shiika Tokuhon* (*The Japanese Poetry Reader*), published by Sanshusha of Tokyo. This volume is a collection of Mr. Ooka's series of nine public lectures on traditional poetry, given as part of a cultural lecture series sponsored by the Yomiuri newspapers in Tokyo.

In translating these chapters we stayed as close as possible to the structure, tone, and wit of the original source material. Mr. Ooka has a well-deserved reputation as a public speaker. So our aim here was to reproduce for an American audience all of the liveliness and flow of his lectures.

THE TRANSLATION OF THE POETRY

Our translations of the poetry in this book were created to reflect Mr. Ooka's readings of the poems. The purpose was to give readers texts in which they could clearly follow Mr. Ooka's interpretations. We hope we have also brought over some of the poems' artistry as well.

The translations are done in free verse because we believe this is the best way to retain the life and flow of the originals. In Japanese the *tanka* verse form of 5, 7, 5, 7, 7 syllables combines with other complex poetic techniques to achieve great compression of meaning. Those other techniques are not available in English, and by itself the *tanka* form is too limiting as a translation medium.

Any translation of this poetry is a contribution to its deeper understanding. There are many other translations the reader may wish to consult. Complete translations of two of the court poetry anthologies have recently appeared: Helen Craig McCullough's *Kokin Wakashu* , *The First Imperial Anthology of Japanese Poetry* (Stanford, California: Stanford University Press, 1989); and Laurel Rasplica Rodd's *Kokinshu, A Collection of Poems Ancient and Modern* (Princeton, New Jersey: Princeton University Press, 1984).

Another valuable source is *Fujiwara Teika's Superior Poems of Our Time* in the well-known translation by Robert H. Brower and Earl Miner (Stanford, California: Stanford University Press, 1967). The only passage in the present volume not written in English by Mr. Ooka or translated by us comes from that book by kind permission of the publisher. It can be found in chapter four.

CONVENTIONS

Certain conventions have been observed throughout this translation.

Personal Names. These follow the Japanese practice: family name first, sometimes followed by *no* (here meaning "belonging to this family"), then given name. This is the reverse of standard English usage. For example: Ki no Tsurayuki (family name Ki, given name Tsurayuki).

Poets' Names. When the full name is not used, we follow the common Japanese form of address for traditional poets and artists, calling them by either their given names, or by the poetic title or pen name associated with them. For example: Ki no Tsurayuki is usually called Tsurayuki; Matsuo Basho is called Basho.

Anthology Names. We use the longer, more correct forms: *Kokin Waka Shu* and *Shin Kokin Waka Shu*. However, the reader should be aware that most of these collections are also commonly known by shorter names: *Kokin Shu* and *Shin Kokin Shu*.

Transliteration. The reader should remember that in Japanese every letter is pronounced. For example, Mr. Ooka's name is pronounced Oh-oka. In one or two cases we have slightly altered the English spelling to avoid confusion or absurdity: for example, *aware* is printed as *awaré* to indicate that it should sound like ah-wah-reh, while Mr. Nose's name is here spelled Nossé, to encourage its pronunciation as Noh-seh.

Acknowledgments

First and foremost, we owe a debt of gratitude to Mr. Ooka for his interest and cooperation in seeing this project through to completion. He not only helped make sure the translation was accurate -- he encouraged us to shape the original to the needs of its intended audience. No translator could ask for more.

We would like to thank Professor Donald Keene of Columbia University most sincerely for his generosity in reading and critiquing the manuscript. We greatly benefited from his deep concern for and unmatched perspective on familiarizing Western readers with Japanese literature. Professor Keene's advice, detailed and to the point, helped us focus on the ultimate purpose of this book.

Our special and deepest thanks are due to Prof. Thomas Fitzsimmons at Oakland University in Michigan. He first encouraged Mr. Ooka to pursue this project as a fellow teacher and a fellow poet. He then gave generously of his time in providing editorial advice on our translations. And finally, he arranged for the publication of this book.

Dr. Janine Beichman of Daito Bunka University in Tokyo found time to offer encouragement and assistance. Her advice helped us in the final revision of the manuscript, particularly the translations of the poetry. We extend her our sincere thanks.

Tanikawa Shuntaro, noted poet, made all this possible by first introducing us to his friend Mr. Ooka. We thank him for his foresight and generosity.

Tokuda Sachiko, our friend in Clifton, NJ, transcribed the tapes Mr. Ooka provided as background and text for this book. Without her help it still might not be done.

Finally, thanks to our children, Mari and Tommy, for their appreciation and forbearance. That's an inspiration in itself.

THE COLORS OF POETRY

Prologue

ON SOME CHARACTERISTICS OF
JAPANESE POETIC CREATION

Seen from the Western world, or by any people geographically distant, Japan today may seem to present two aspects which no stretch of the imagination can join. One is of course an astonishing technological manipulative development covering the many fields of science and industry; while the other, typically represented by Zen, is a non-manipulative discipline which can be considered one of the most developed forms of meditation. There exists on the one hand an economy which incessantly progresses and surprises, and on the other the dedicated pursuit of the Immutable through time.

Noticing these two aspects does not of course explain or even express the galaxy of accomplishments in present-day Japan, particularly in what concerns culture. And just as in all the other arts, the central fact about contemporary Japanese poetry is that it is an ensemble of differing, often daring, not to say chaotic attempts to penetrate and to explore.

In this crucible many currents come together, some in harmony, others at odds. Not only does the new confront the old, sometimes the new confronts itself. These confrontations are often found in the same poet.

In attempting to sort out the situation in Japanese poetry I shall divide my remarks into two parts. First I will give you a short-hand historical perspective on the three modes used by poets in Japan today, the traditional *haiku* and *waka* and the modern *gendai-shi*. I will describe the outstanding characteristics of these modes as well their present condition in Japan.

Secondly I will look into the special character of Japanese poetic creation, focusing especially on how from ancient times to the present there has been a strong tendency toward both making and appreciating poetry collectively. And here I shall share with you, and this may interest even those among you who have little interest in poetry as such, the deep essential connections between Japanese poetry and daily life.

While calling attention throughout to the interplay of old and new, and to the resulting complexities in the work, I shall emphasize four general characteristics of Japanese poetry:

1) its intimate involvement with the details of daily life and its consequent "earthliness;"

2) its dynamic role as a force in the society and as a presence in the experience of the people;

3) the resulting tension it reveals between the claims of the mundane and of the elevated or refined; and, within that tension,

4) the continuing interplay, sometimes struggle, between the "banquet" of communal involvement and the private vision of the "solitary mind."

Haiku or *haikai* have for a long time figured in every poetic list addressed to the foreign reader. It has become popular in the United States to write and appreciate the short poems inspired by the form, and major 20th century French poets like Jean Cocteau and Paul Eluard have left short poems which reflect clearly the interest brought to *haiku*. It is a special form that characterized the finest Japanese poetic expression, and its extreme brevity justifies the curiosity which it evokes.

Within its strict limit of seventeen syllables this traditional form translates fleeting or momentary impressions of existence, as well as sensations and subtle vibrations of the spirit, as the poet finds himself before the most imperceptible changes of the climate and the seasons. Thus *haiku* might be called a poetic sketch, drawn with the delicate strokes of a sensitive brush, that characterizes the Japanese spirit.

This ability to discern the least vibrations of the cosmos through the simplest changes of daily life is precisely what has guaranteed centuries of long life to this poetic strategy, probably the most condensed in the world. The great mystic poet William Blake one day summed up as his aspiration "to see the World in a grain of sand." Matsuo Basho, the greatest *haiku* poet, who lived in the 17th century, would have completely agreed with this sentiment. But what seems to me more important is the fact that this attitude, this sensibility which resonates more than ever when faced with the ephemeral, is the most natural manner of perception among Japanese classical poets.

There exists another classical form of poetry in Japan: *waka*, or as it is generally called now, *tanka*.

Composed of thirty-one syllables, it is a form found in Japanese literature for over a thousand years and still flourishing. It constitutes, with *haiku*, Japan's most popular poetic expression.

Though *haiku* might be far better known to foreign readers, it is very important to acknowledge that *waka* (*tanka*) has been the fundamental poetic form throughout the long tradition of Japanese poetry. Indeed, the form of *haiku* is derived from that of *waka*.

The essence of *waka* comes out of those sensations we feel in everyday life. Especially important themes include:
1) love between men and women (scarcely treated in *haiku* except in the derivative form *senryu*);
2) deep attachment to nature, in the joys and sorrows experienced face to face with each detail of the changing seasons;
3) celebration and mourning for those with whom the poet has a close relationship, including seasonal greetings of a very sophisticated or witty kind;
4) sincere and deep reflections on miscellaneous aspects of one's life.

While *haiku* can be called the crystallization of fugitive instants, one might call *waka* or *tanka* the endless lyrical stream of sentiments and thoughts experienced in everyday life.

Contemporary poetry is a new kind of writing that differs from both *tanka* and *haiku*. Having come into existence nearly a century ago, and having no fixed form comparable to *tanka* or *haiku*, it has as its aim the free translation of meditations, complex feelings, and a variety of observations which give personality to the modern age. The abundance of response here is difficult to contain in the condensed forms of *tanka* and *haiku*.

Post-romantic poetry, the theater, and the epic poems of Europe played a leading role in the creation and development of this new genre; the century-long history of Japanese modern poetry is characterized by considerable influences from Western literature.

It is not easy to evaluate in what measure the compact, dense, and sophisticated structure of sensibility which Europe hammered out over the centuries could have been transplanted to and taken root in the mental climate of Japan, where modernization signified Europeanization pure and simple, and has from the beginning often been manifested superficially as imitation or plagiarism.

Nevertheless it remains true and is obvious that, even when placed in such a peculiar set of historical circumstances, every poet is in a position to hold onto his personal world, and to express that world with the aid of the new forms that influence him. Such poets as Takamura Kotaro (1883-1956) or Hagiwara Sakutaro (1886-1942) worked out the line which this new poetry was to take.

While *tanka* and *haiku* kept to the traditional forms, this new genre has had recourse to a "free verse" with no fixed prosody, and its vast extent includes ideological and lyric poems as well as dramatic poetry and prose-poems. Situated in an international framework, such contemporary Japanese poetry gradually affirmed its own existence in a climate of Symbolism. The works of Baudelaire, Mallarmé, Rimbaud and Verlaine were quickly translated and acquired admirers. In accordance with the introduction of the idea of democracy, Whitman's humanism and praise of the people influenced the literary world of Japan. The nature-cult of a Wordsworth or a Thoreau and the mystical conceptions of a Blake or a Tagore also attracted disciples.

Nevertheless we see in even the most modern poetry a traditionally deep tendency to express one's own feelings and thoughts as a modern man or woman from a modernized society in some very stylized way influenced by the long tradition of *tanka* and *haiku*.

In other words, just as in other areas of Japanese life, in modern poetry there persists a variety of elements from ancient and traditional forms, and into these have been thickly mixed the different experiments of the avant-garde. Thus contemporary Japanese poetry comes into being full of diversity.

There are now in Japan four magazines, three monthly and one quarterly, devoted to modern poetry. They are sold all over the country and enjoy a certain commercial success. In addition there are three or four hundred small publications which poets publish individually or collectively at their own cost. Some of these appear regularly every month and can count on a few hundred subscriptions each. The majority are non-periodic, irregular publications which often disappear after a few years. The activities of these mini-reviews are not to be ignored, for they often introduce young poets of talent.

Poetry reading in public places also is developing year by year, though the audience is still limited.

In the case of *tanka* and *haiku* there are six large monthly periodicals that sell from several thousand to several tens of thousands of copies apiece. These are surrounded by mini-journals, in greater numbers than those devoted to contemporary poetry.

It is quite clear then that the Japanese love to write and read poetry. It is also true, and very important to keep in mind, that the mainstream of this poetry focuses on the small discoveries of daily life, or on the expression of subtle sensations evoked by seasonal changes.

Now if by the word *poet* we understand a mouthpiece of the supernatural and transcendent Being, one whose words should always be urgent appeals or extraordinary revelations from the fearsome "other-world," then we will not understand the nature of traditional Japanese poetry or of the Japanese poet.

For a traditional Japanese person poetry is first of all a means of expressing intimate and familiar facts. There is no question of a dramatic dialogue bridging a terrifying distance between man and the superhuman; rather there is a wink of complicity, an expression of mutual comprehension between fellow humans, and between man and the things that surround him.

Japanese poetry is essentially *earthly*.

I wish to quote here from the French novelist and critic André Malraux. In his small book *Une esquisse pour la psychologie du Cinéma* (1939), one of the preparatory works for his *Les Voix du Silence*, he says, concerning the contribution of Christianity to European painting: "In the world of pictures, in which there was hardly anything more than somewhat subtly symbolic representation, Christianity introduced dramatic representations, previously unknown. Buddhism has its scenes, but no drama.... Europe substituted contrast for unity of tone, history for annals, drama for tragedy, romance for the tale, psychology for wisdom, action for contemplation: man for the gods."

This remark seems significant to me even in thinking about the characteristics of Japanese poetry. Actually one can say in general that in the Japanese soul "this fanatic need for the object, essential to the Occident and related to its political conquest of the world" (Malraux) rarely can be found. For many Japanese thinking about poetry and writing poems both demand a state of soul to which this "fanatic need" is alien.

These things being said, I wish to examine more specifically the characteristics of Japanese poetic creation.

I have long been interested in the fact that in the Japanese arts, as well as such hobbies as flower arranging, the tea ceremony, and the like, one clear tendency or principle can be seen. It is the liking people have for calling together their comrades and forming "associations" (*kessha*), "coterie magazines" (*dojin-zasshi*), and "art groups" (*bijutsu dantai*), as well as the various schools of flower arranging, tea ceremony, and the like.

Even people who identify themselves as avant-garde call together their avant-garde comrades and form groups. Soon, in many cases, they become so at ease with one another they lose the habit of critical interest in each other's work and the power of destruction characteristic of the avant garde.

Why is it that the Japanese so much like to gather together? It is easy to look down upon this psychological tendency, as Japanese intellectuals themselves so frequently do. But since even those intellectuals often rest at ease within their own group, their critique of the situation occasionally becomes comical.

I think it is insufficient to examine this phenomenon from a negative point of view only. Let me give you some positive aspects.

In associations for *tanka* and *haiku* there may be several thousand members under one leader or director, and among the members there will be several ranks. General members will each month send a fixed number of *tanka* or *haiku* to their leader and he will correct them; then, having selected a few poems, he will publish them in the association's monthly magazine. The meaning of the word "correct" (*ten-saku*) here is to make additions (*ten*) and subtractions (*saku*), or in short "to make modifications."

If we take the position that poetry is the single expression of an individual's thought and emotion, such examples of writers of modern verse submitting to "modification" of their work will probably seem difficult to understand. But the reality is that several tens of thousands of people recognize such methods as positively valuable.

We may say they enjoy participating in the "virtues of form." That the same can be said about tea, or flower arranging, or calligraphy will be immediately recognized by anyone who knows even a little about these activities.

I have for a long time been interested in the uniquely Japanese nature of this custom. Gradually I have begun to realize that it is something rooted in the most essential aspect of literature and the arts in Japan. I investigated this notion with regard to classical poetry and recently published a book entitled *Utage to Koshin* (*The Banquet and the Solitary Mind*). It perhaps goes without saying that the word *utage* ("banquet") in the title indicates the tendency of Japanese to gather together in the sense just described.

The *utage* originally had the meaning of like-minded people holding a banquet for enjoyment. But I thought that it could also be used in speaking of the history of Japanese poetry.

In ancient Japan there was a linked history of Imperial anthologies compiled by one or more poets who, commissioned by the Emperor and working in his stead, chose the most famous verses of past and present. These anthologies set the standard of taste in the world of poetry. Around the 9th century there were even compiled several Imperial anthologies of Chinese verse written by the Japanese.

The motive behind the compilation of these anthologies seems to have been the desire to celebrate the peace and prosperity of such and such an Emperor's reign. The most polished expression of that celebration would be a collection of poetry. In other words, the Imperial anthologies of Chinese and Japanese verse were splendid "banquets" of language given over to celebration and salutation.

From a point of view which values the uniqueness and purity of individual expression such poetry will be considered poor stuff. Yet such works as *Kokin Waka Shu* (*An Anthology of Verse Past and Present*), collected at the beginning of the 10th century, and *Shin Kokin Waka Shu* (*A New Anthology of Verse Past and Present*), in the 13th century, represent the highest point of literary expression in their respective periods. As such they deeply influenced later generations.

Kokin Waka Shu had a huge influence, extending beyond later poetic developments to affect the customs, manners, and daily interests and tastes of the Japanese.

I wonder if this is not a phenomenon unique to Japan.

The principle of the "banquet" has been working vigorously in the various forms which make up the main streams of Japanese classical poetry: in *uta-awase* (poetry contest), in *renga* (linked verse), and in *haikai no renga* (a developed form of linked verse). All of these works of poetry are made and appreciated and evaluated not in the closed room of the individual but in the context of a group. And that this tradition has come down to the present in the manner I described earlier is, I think, beyond doubt.

Poetry -- it is sad this cannot be said of the present -- poetry in ancient times, and for a long time, was what determined the basic forms of the people's esthetic consciousness. The fact that in poetry this principle of the banquet was working so vigorously meant that inevitably its influence would extend to other areas of daily life.

For example, in order to ornament or decorate *byobu* (a folding screen -- a piece of interior furniture), people would not only draw pictures on the screen, but would also paste on it pieces of beautiful paper onto which poems had been written to harmonize with the pictures.

They sought to arrange a kind of "banquet" of pictures and poems. While people gazed upon and appreciated the screen they also made new poems. Others made another kind of picture, *emaki* (picture scrolls), in which they depicted the appearance of the room where the screen stood. In this manner the setting of the *utage* or banquet led to new associations and gradually spread. Thus the beautification of daily life advanced to its most extreme forms.

Various kinds of amusements which involve the comparison of levels of taste also were born out of this setting. *E-awase* (picture competitions), *kai-awase* (shell competitions), *kusa-awase* (herb competitions) -- are all of this kind. The poetry cards known as the *hyakunin isshu* (one hundred poems of a hundred poets), even now a form of amusement at New Year's, are nothing other than a "banquet" where one plays with an anthology of one hundred outstanding verses.

If I were to summarize what I have said in one expression, it would be "the transformation of life into art." What we should take note of is that in traditional Japan this kind of "transformation of life into art" always had poetry, that is to say *waka* or *tanka* as well as *haiku*, as its companion. If one looks at this situation from the side of *waka* poetry it is nothing other than "the application of poetry to real life," or in other words "the practicalization of art." And the fact is that as this tendency advances, poetry (*waka*) becomes mixed into the daily customs and manners of the people, and its quality rapidly declines.

As a result, within the daily life of the Japanese, stereotyped *waka*-like sentiments, even though they are fragmented and their original form is lost, everywhere remain. In daily life when least expected they float to the surface of people's spirit. We can see this aspect frequently exploited to produce sentimental or lyrical effects in the *yakuza-eiga* (gangster movies) as well as in movies called avant-garde.

"The transformation of life into art," or "the practicalization of art" -- it is here, I believe, that we find the fundamental motive of those huge numbers of people who form and support the *tanka* and *haiku* associations, and the flower arranging, tea, and calligraphy associations of modern Japan, and now even of America. It is a phenomenon with a very ancient history.

But, as I just said, the "banquet" tradition also almost inevitably produces a tendency to drown *waka* or *haiku* poetry in the customs and manners of daily life.

And it is at this point that in every crucial period in the history of Japan a burning desire to save poetry from the mundane and to make it again shine forth and be valued as poetry captures the imagination of outstanding poets, and a new age of poetry begins.

The high points of the history of poetry in Japan have been the achievement of such poets. I have called their burning desire *koshin* (the solitary mind).

What I find extremely interesting is that only those poets who are aware of the "solitary mind" and remain faithful to their personal fate (which makes their return to the solitary mind inevitable) while keeping a place within the "banquet," only those poets produce works at which we stare in wonder. Yet if they cut themselves off from the world of the "banquet" and withdraw into the solitary mind alone, their works mysteriously lose power.

Between the will which seeks to participate in the world of the "banquet" (the world of the collective spiritual body) and the will which seeks to devote itself purely to the self (the world of the solitary mind) there is tension. As long as this tension is present the works which the poets produce give off their highest luster. This is, to my mind, so central an aspect of the reality of Japanese poetry, both modern and traditional, that it can never be emphasized enough.

Chapter One

TRANSCENDING COLOR

For the ancient Japanese the word "color," *iro*, evoked the idea of time passing, of change with its multifold meanings. The *Iwanami Classical Dictionary* defines the word as follows:

> Originally hue, complexion. Hence, beautiful coloring, as of a woman's appearance.
> Desire, in the sense of attraction to the above.
> Woman, prostitute, or lover as the object of desire.
> Also, from hue -- color of feelings, mood, looks, premonition.
> The word is also used as an equivalent of the Buddhist *shiki* (aspect, matter).

In its nuance of "beautiful" hues *iro* instantly suggests beauty that fades, or feelings that are inconstant.

The Origin of Kanji by Kato Joken goes deeper, basing its reading on the adopted Chinese character the Japanese use to write the word:

> The ideogram shows two people grappling with each other and becoming one. It explicitly shows intercourse. Hence *iro* came to mean "woman" because the object of man's desire is woman; thence derives "face" because woman's face is beautiful; and further it came to mean beautiful colors.

A Dictionary of the Origins of Kanji, by Todo Akiyasu, gives a similar definition:

> A compound formation of two characters: one person with another, showing the condition of a man's intercourse with a woman. *Iro* in the sense of desire is the original meaning and the meaning "colors" is merely its derivative.

The actual ideogram for *iro* (色) represents a person kneeling, with another person riding on top.

At first glance all of classical Japanese poetry seems immersed in color. As early as *Kokin Waka Shu* (905 A.D.), however, in a preface written in native Japanese script (a conscious departure from the practice of using Chinese for official documents), we read:

> As the world now is obsessed with color, and people's hearts are fickle as flowers, only idle songs and mutable matters abound. And even they are left unheeded, buried in the dwelling-place of desire. So native poetry can hardly be brought out in public on serious occasions. If we consider the origins of poetry this should not be so.

Here colors and flowers are condemned as undesirable. The author (this preface is attributed to Ki no Tsurayuki) fervently believed that native poetry (*waka*) would again reach the elevated position it held during the *Man'yo Shu* (760 A.D.) period, when it played a role in official public celebrations.

Completion of the court-sponsored anthology *Kokin Waka Shu* actually represented the realization of his hopes. His preface communicates his distress over native poetry's inferior position up to then, and triumph over the renewed recognition of its merit. He denounces the contemporary state of *waka* as being "buried in the dwelling-place of desire" and "obsessed with color." He wants to release *waka* from its exclusive use as a means of personal communication between lovers, and he hopes to see it regain the position of official respectability which Chinese forms had monopolized for 100 years.

Here we see the word *iro* (color) used to imply such states of mind as happiness, amorous sentiment, and desire. Conversely, what is considered desirable would naturally assume pleasant colors, so one cannot separate the sense of "color" from that of amorous sentiment.

Iro, then, communicates both color and feeling. When we read "the world now is obsessed with color," we can think of a world where "sex" and "color" are inseparable twin fixations.

And Tsurayuki's statement on poetry can be read as his criticism of the society he saw about him.

THE MAN'YO SENSE OF COLOR

The peach, the favorite tree of Chinese poets during the T'ang dynasty, will help us understand the two meanings of color.

We find many flowering trees in T'ang poetry, and not many flowering plants. Most of the tree references concern peaches, plums, *ume* (Japanese apricots), and apricots. It is interesting to note that all these trees are loved as much for their edible fruit as for their beautiful flowers.

We soon realize, however, that the floral tastes of the T'ang Chinese and the ancient Japanese were quite different. True, the Japanese loved the blossoms of the *ume*, the orange, and the cherry trees. But if all the references to flowers in Japanese poetry collections since the *Man'yo Shu* anthology of 760 A.D. were added up, there would be more mentions of flowering plants than of flowering trees.

Still, *Man'yo Shu* is liberally planted with trees. It mentions 66 flowering trees, four bamboos, and 83 flowering plants, according to Maeda Yukichika's study *Murasakikusa*. Even larger numbers of flowering plants may appear in later collections. It is noteworthy, then, that peaches and plums, the Chinese favorites, but particularly the peach tree, did not seem to hold much attraction for the Japanese.

Maeda also says that 502 of the poems in *Man'yo Shu* mention flowers. The three floral colors most frequently cited are white (in 204 verses), purple and light purple (137), and red and pink (93).

White, represented mainly by *ume* and orange blossoms, leads by a wide margin over the pink of cherry and peach blossoms. *Ume* was a newly imported tree and so might have excited the *modernisme* of the people of the Man'yo era. Maeda points out that the poetry about cherry blossoms is superior to the poetry about *ume* in complexity, delicacy, and sublimity, and that cherry blossoms seem to occupy a loftier position in the poets' subconscious.

Of the two Chinese imports, *ume* and the peach, *ume* was almost an object of adoration, while the peach was given limited attention.

> The Chinese taste in flowers is obvious in the way they took pleasure in peach and plum blossoms, especially deep pink ones. They talked of "crimson flowers and green willows," and the flowers always seemed to be represented as crimson.... It was natural for the Chinese people to have a taste for such flowers, as they lived in houses decorated in red, green and other bright colors, and wore red and green clothes. Some [Japanese] seem to think that the Chinese love only orchids and bamboo, but this is a total misconception. In paintings, too, the Chinese paint flowers and birds because of their voluptuous colors.
>
> (Tsuda Sokichi, "Flowers and Wines in Chinese Poetry," *The Study of Japanese Literature*)

In *Murasakikusa*, in the chapter "Heian Culture and Red Dye," Maeda describes how red dye, which was not popular at all in the Nara period (710-794 A.D.), suddenly became so popular during the Heian period (794-1192 A.D.) that courtiers flocked to wear red clothing. There was even an ordinance restricting certain colors to certain ranks and forbidding the wearing of red clothing by lower-rank courtiers.

This extravagance in fashion did help refine Japanese culture. It also invited a decadence so severe it eroded the economic position of at least a part of the Heian aristocracy, which spent enormous sums on the fad. But while red quickly gained acceptance in daily life, in poetry its acceptance does not seem to have been quite so simple.

Let us turn for a moment to the Genroku and Hoei reigns of the Edo period (1688-1710). *Selected Writings in Manners*, edited by Morikawa Kyoriku, a disciple of Basho, has a chapter "On a Hundred Flowers," written by the editor himself, in which he speaks of the peach in these terms:

> The peach is fundamentally a vulgar tree. It has none of the air of elegance of *ume* or cherry blossoms. It is like a low class child, all decked out for a festive occasion, clad in the only fine outfit she owns. In the midst of this blossoming flourish her lowliness is betrayed by the fuzz along her nape and behind her ears.

The wit in this put-down is original enough, but the idea that peaches are "vulgar", both in class and taste, was not necessarily Kyoriku's own. We find the following dialogue in the *Joruri* (musical narrative) for Chikamatsu Hanji's puppet play *Tale of a Three Day Peace*, staged at the Takemoto theater in the 1760's, the middle Edo period.

> Just look at these trees! Everyone praises cherry blossoms as if they were the only flower, and slights the peach. But in full bloom, peach blossoms are far superior to *ume* and cherry. Isn't this a wonderful sight?
>
> It certainly is. I've heard of this peach orchard's beauty, but this is the first time I've seen it. I think of it as a gentle girl. Even you couldn't guess how I feel inside -- wanting to pick an adorable twig, yet afraid I'd be accused of violating her in front of all these witnesses.

Here too, as Kyoriku points out, peach blossoms are somewhat flushed and sensual in spite of themselves. Their voluptuousness was scorned precisely for its easy allure.

A long time span separates this era from the age of the preface to *Kokin Waka Shu*. Yet we can easily see the close kinship between the feeling, expressed here, that peach blossoms are vulgar, and Tsurayuki's sentiment in scorning a "world now . . . obsessed with color."

Peach blossoms and cherry blossoms are two distinct shades of pink. There is ample room for sensory distinctions between the two. To Japanese writers the peach blossom evokes a plump, voluptuously sexy woman, while the cherry blossom with its multi-layered petals projects the image of a woman whose exquisite slimness is heightened by her dress.

COLOR AND OBJECT

A survey of the manifestation of color in Japanese poetry makes it clear that the Japanese seldom perceive colors in an exclusively visual way. Their perception of color is more tactile, or filtered through some tactile impression.

For though it seems that Japanese literature usually portrays a rich chromatic range, on closer examination we find surprisingly few direct references to colors. Instead the names of natural objects, especially plants, appear in such a way that we react to them as colors. The impression of a rich palette comes from writers pointing at things instead of directly at their colors. Rather than say lavender, for example, we invoke thoroughwort, *hagi* (Japanese bush clover), or arrowroot. In place of yellow we mention globeflower, *ominaeshi*, chrysanthemum. For pink we have wild pink, peach blossom, cherry blossom, mallow, peony, silk tree, knotwood. For red we name camellias or lilies; for purple, wisteria, violets, iris. Blue will be suggested by Chinese bell flowers, morning-glories, hydrangeas, gentians; white by *ume*, chrysanthemum, orange blossom, Japanese sunflowers (*deutzia*).

This practice is not limited to plant colors. Pigments are also called by the names of their source materials.

These colors are inseparable from the texture of natural objects. They are not abstractions, but basic attributes of the natural objects. As a result, right from antiquity the range of direct color-denoting adjectives in the Japanese language has been highly restricted.

Originally the Japanese language only had words for the color concepts of white, black, red, and blue. Yellow was added later. For centuries these were the only abstract color adjectives in the language. Furthermore, in antiquity each of the adjectives white, black, blue, and red was used to denote a wide range of colors, so the adjectives were quite limited in their function as qualifiers. (See "The Nature of Color-Indicative Vocabulary in Ancient Japanese," in Satake Akihiro's *Man'yo Shu Bassho*.)

Carmine, dry leaves, porcelain blue, light scallion, crested ibis (damask), bush warbler (brownish green), gardenia, rust red -- in ancient times the Japanese language specified an enormous number of colors. Its very richness stuns us. But in a sense this development was natural, a matter of course. To discover an object in nature was to discover its color. Logically, the number of colors could match the number of known natural objects.

Is this precise observation? Or simple thoughtlessness?

It takes an acute and refined sensitivity to name an object, then to make that name designate a color. For this feat we can credit the precise sensory awareness of the Japanese. On the other hand, the Japanese never attempted to create an abstract conception of color embodied in a spectrum to classify delicate differences of shades. This suggests some peculiarities in the Japanese conception of things.

It may be that from earliest times the Japanese never really saw color in its relationship to light. This, at least, is what the poetry from *Man'yo Shu* to *Shin Kokin Waka Shu* suggests. Rarely is there a kinetic and impressionistic grasp of color as a function of light.

There are some prophetic pieces, of course, such as this one by Fujiwara Teika.

> *Kurenai no tsuyu ni asahi o utsushimote*
> *atari made teru nadeshiko no hana*

> The wild pink
> spreads its glow
> its crimson dew
> holding the morning sun

And later collections of poetry present a group of poets who demonstrate a tenuous, sketchy, but quite impressionistic grasp of nature.

> *Mahagi chiru niwa no akikaze mi ni shimite*
> *yuhi no kage zo kabe ni kieyuku*

> In the yard where the bush clover sheds its petals
> the autumn wind of weariness
> chills me through
> The sinking sun's glow
> seeps into the wall
>   *Eifuku mon-in*

> *Murasame no nakaba hareyuku kumokiri ni*
> *aki no hi kiyoki matsubara no yama*

> The passing shower starts to clear
> dissipating clouds and mist

A clean autumn day rests
on the Matsubara mountains

Hanazono-in

These poems demonstrate a grasp of nature in the course of change. They foreshadow the treatment of nature characteristic of the later *renga* (linked verse). Perhaps as poets understood more clearly how the perception of natural objects changes constantly under the influence of light, the 31 syllables of *tanka* became less adequate to express what they saw.

COLORLESSNESS AS A PRIMARY COLOR

Japanese poets often treat light as a tangible substance. "The sinking sun's glow" in the poem just quoted (the Japanese phrase can also mean "the shadow of the evening sun") does not fade away on the surface of the wall -- it actually seeps into that wall. When ex-Emperor Hanazono says "A clean autumn day rests," it is most certainly not a simple visual observation. The core of the expression is a tactile reaction to the clear, chilly autumn air after a passing shower.

This tactile response, so familiar to the *Shin Kokin Waka Shu* poets, was also known to the earlier poets of the *Kokin Waka Shu*.

The sensory touch of Oshikochi no Mitsune, for example, one of the editors of *Kokin Waka Shu*, especially impresses me. He was one of the eight representative poets of his time who gathered for a poetry-composing party at Ki no Tsurayuki's house. The poets sat along a stream, down which a cup floated. Each had to finish a poem before the cup reached him. Tsurayuki and his guests were all presumably in their late twenties.

They were assigned three themes: flowers floating on water in the Spring; water reflecting a hanging lantern; and the moon hiding among flowers, darkening the pool. All eight poets composed one piece each on every one of the assigned themes.

Mitsune's piece on flowers floating on water in the Spring reads:

*Yamigakure iwama o wakete yuku mizu no
koe sae hana no ka nizo shimikeru.*

Hidden by the dark
the water streams among rocks
Even its sound is soaked with
the scent of cherry blossoms

It's an extraordinary sensitivity that can feel the scent of cherry blossoms saturating the sound of water. Such a sense of "saturation" is a clear and constant factor in the history of Japanese poetry. Compare a poem by Fujiwara Shunzei, from the *Shin Kokin Waka Shu* era:

Yu sareba nobe no akikaze mi ni shimite
uzura nakunari fukakusa no sato.

As evening comes
autumn winds over the field
chill me through
Quails call in this village of rank grass

Shunzei presents this sense of saturation (by the chill) as a simple tactile experience.

But later, during his son Fujiwara Teika's time, we have:

Shirotae no sode no wakare ni tsuyu ochite
mi ni shimu iro no akikaze zo fuku

We part in tears
dew falling on our white sleeves
The wind of autumn, of weariness
carries the color that seeps into me

Here the autumn wind takes on a "color that seeps into" him. The sensory experience is internalized. Incidentally, lest anyone misunderstand, this is a love poem.

Teika also wrote:

> *Kiewabinu utsurou hito no aki no iro ni*
> *mi o kogarashi no mori no shita tsuyu.*

> I am like dew on the underbrush
> blown, consumed by my longing
> My lover is drifting away
> I wish to disappear, but in vain
> in the color of autumn, of weariness

"Color" here transcends all common colors. Yet in these poems I feel the color of Japanese poetry very strongly. This color is, so to speak, a "colorless primary color." It is an absolute, a conscious abstraction from the colors that adhere to natural objects in the world.

Seeing color in the wind is a function not of the visual sense but of the mind's eye. It is one's heart that sees color in the wind. This is far removed from any perception of the actual physical aspects of color. It is a vision not rooted in natural causes, but one growing from an act of the will. The poets had colorful objects in plenty to look at in their daily lives: clothes, furniture, the interiors of temples, vegetation. By denying the physical colors of their lives, they sought to develop a penetrating eye that would let them see the color of colorless objects.

This effort is rooted in the Buddhist idea that "all (color) is vanity." Fujiwara Shunzei makes the connection clear in a poem, written after *Hokkekyo* (the Saddharmapundarika sutra), which promulgates this teaching of the Buddha:

> *Takasago no Onoe no sakura mishikoto mo*
> *omoeba kanashi iro ni medekeru*

> How we viewed
> the time honored cherry blossoms at Onoe
> Thinking back, it is so sad --
> how we reveled in color

But in another poem, similarly didactic, he wrote of the radiant shore of the heavenly world that the diligent practitioner of Buddhism might see. In the preface to that poem he writes, "As it dawns, the sound of the waves surges toward the golden shore." The poem reads:

> *Inishie no Onoe no kane ni nitarukana*
> *kishi utsu nami no akatsuki no koe*

> It sounds like the temple bell in Onoe
> in ancient times
> the voice of the dawn, the waves
> beating on the shore

This poem makes no direct reference to colors, yet we can feel a golden radiance filling the air.

BEYOND VULGARITY IN POETRY

We have seen that by the time of *Shin Kokin Waka Shu* Japanese poetry had positively established the colors of the mind as separate and distinct from the colors of individual objects. This idea was already germinating when Tsurayuki lamented that the people of his time were "obsessed with color," and Basho later advocated the same viewpoint when he upheld truth through refinement.

This view embodies the anti-vulgarism of Japanese poetry. It explains why Japanese poetry as a whole, seemingly so full of flourishes and elegant elements, has persisted in its single-minded pursuit of cold, desolate mental states. It reveals the asceticism behind the poetic opposition to vulgarity.

The Japanese poets' pursuit of a color that physically "seeps" into things may have the same root as their unwillingness to be satisfied with the merely visual aspects of color.

Shinkei's *Sasamegoto* (*Trivia*) records a conversation between Teika and his father, Shunzei. It is an episode probably retold from Teika's so-called forged documents, which are nevertheless considered to be of extraordinary importance.

Teika told his father that his (Teika's) poetry had been widely praised as gentle and elegant up through his thirties, but in his forties it was seen as bony, insufficiently refined. This had caused his fame to wane. How should he train himself?

Shunzei answered, "You did well to think things through this far and ask me this question. There's no cause to lament.

"In spite of myself, my style is flesh alone. But you very naturally get to the bones in your poetry. I envy your poetry a great deal.... To get to the bones of the matter is the supreme concern."

Moved to tears, Shunzei continued, "If you keep on going the way you are, you will be the best poet in the world."

A commendation of "boniness" from Shunzei, a poet who pursued the world of mystic elegance, is quite striking. Similarly, Shinkei elsewhere agrees with an ancient poet's metaphor to describe what poetry should be: "like filling a crystal with lapis lazuli." Then he adds his own note: "cold and clear."

The implication of sensory grasp is consistent. He reaffirms it when, commenting on an ancient poet's line "like pouring water over a five-foot-tall iris," he notes: "shiny wet and stretched out."

Living in the midst of color, the Japanese poet concentrates on trying to transcend it. Having staked his truth on negating the vulgar, he proceeds on the basis of an acutely developed inner sensory perception. This attitude contains the color of Japanese poetry itself, and offers opportunities for a peculiarly Japanese symbolism.

Chapter Two

SLEEPING ALONE

We have seen how Japanese poetry at its best is characterized by a singular inner organic sense. The poetry consistently strives to penetrate the surface. As a linguistic manifestation of this process, let us look at how the Japanese use the word *shimiru*, "to penetrate."

Shimiru comes from the verb *shimu*. As an intransitive verb, *shimu* means to absorb color, to be penetrated. It applies to the absorption of color or fragrance, and to the soaking up of water. It also implies taking something to heart. In its transitive form *shimu* means to dye, dip, or dip into dye (see "Ancient Era" in Sanseido's *A Comprehensive Dictionary of the Japanese Language by Historical Periods*).

So a word that originally meant "to dye" broadened to mean "to absorb or be penetrated by fragrance or water," and then "to take something to heart." From this last meaning came the adverb shimijimi, describing the feeling of holding something deep in one's heart. This process shows how the ancient Japanese, so well acquainted with natural plant dyes, refined their perceptions.

The feeling of *shimiru* certainly plays a large role in the situation of lovers, two of whom, as we have seen, are described as forming the ideogram for the word *iro* (color).

When lovers meet feelings naturally run deep, and when they are apart *shimiru* is present in each of them individually. Hence the word *shimijimi*, implying a sense of internalized closeness.

In both senses the word also conveys the meaning of "taking on color." It appears quite frequently in Japanese love poetry, and its prominence is significant.

Poems about love and being in love make up a large part of classical Japanese poetry. The love poems in *Man'yo Shu* are superb in quantity and quality. In *Kokin Waka Shu*, the original court-sponsored poetry anthology that became a model for all later anthologies, five of the twenty volumes concern love, and love-related poems are found in the anthology's seasonal and miscellaneous sections as well.

THE IMAGINATION IN JAPANESE AND WESTERN LOVE POETRY

Before I examine some ancient and medieval Japanese love poems I would like to make a personal observation on the differences between Japanese and Western love poetry.

The "Song of Love and Joy" by Ghazar Sebastatsi, the 16th century Armenian poet of the Southern Caucasus, has a sanctified lover as its unifying image. Sebastatsi uses this figure for the same basic purpose as Dante the Florentine uses the image of Beatrice in *The Divine Comedy*. The glorification and mystification of woman, epitomized in the Madonna worship nurtured by the Catholic church, is visible in both the rural Armenian poet and the cosmopolitan Dante.

Love is a fundamental passion, common to all mankind, rooted in our basic reproductive instinct. But it manifests itself in many ways. Each society accepts, then modifies and expresses love according to its language, customs, and manners. A culture expresses itself in the way it manifests love.

Naturally religion figures significantly in the process. Think, for example, of how love and the reproductive instinct are modified and expressed within a specific racial environment when native beliefs merge with a universal religion such as Buddhism, Christianity, or Islam. (The fusion of Shinto with Buddhism in Japan is one of many such cases.) This factor alone could make the expression of love multifaceted and idiosyncratic.

Here is part of Sebastatsi's poem:

> The moon and the sun came down from the sky
> and hung in your hair so tenderly
> Your forehead is adorned with stars
> Like them I burn, intoxicated with love

. . . .
Your breasts like the moon
are the cross offered in thanks to God
I your pilgrim
bearing candles and censer
with my arms held out to the sky I pray to you
Your grace pierces me, my pain is no more

This celebration of a woman is the product of a distinctly Western imagination. In how many among the great number of Japanese poems do we find a woman celebrated in this way, presented as having the moon and sun hung in her hair, her forehead beaded with stars? Almost none, I am sure.

It is quite strange -- or perhaps, come to think of it, entirely natural -- that the presentation of woman in love poems should reveal so clearly the differences between the making of poetry in Japan and the West, and between the philosophical views of man and woman in each culture.

Cross-cultural traffic between East and West, North and South, continues to increase as time goes on. We share our influences, and our ways of thinking and feeling seem to be moving closer together. But under the surface things are not that simple. We see more and more evidence of complexity and difference.

If Sebastatsi's poem were presented to us as Dante's, we might accept it without much question. But if it were presented as Ariwara no Narihira's, or Fujiwara Teika's, for example, we would laugh in disbelief. Western long poems are completely different in form from *waka*, of course, so any comparison between them is essentially impossible. But excluding the question of poetic form, my point here is that Western and Japanese poets lived in worlds that were fundamentally different. The difference is clearly revealed in the way they adore, worship, express and celebrate a loved one.

Put more plainly, their creativity is rooted in their social origins, including assumptions about the relationship between man and woman prevalent in their respective societies.

In Sebastatsi a woman is a universe, a symbol of great nature herself. She has attributes of the Virgin Mary, the most significant female figure in Christianity. In this she manifests the power of the Catholic church, influential from the Middle Ages through the Renaissance and right into modern times. The poet calls the moon-like mounds of her breasts "the cross offered . . . to

God". He calls himself a "pilgrim." When he prays to her, "with my arms held out to the sky," her "grace" pierces him, and his "pain is no more." In other words, he is no more than a "slave" to the glorious woman he loves.

EGOCENTRISM IN JAPANESE LOVE POETRY

Such mystical glorification of women is almost completely absent in Japanese love poetry. We do find gushing confessions of fervent love, but throughout their work Japanese poets share one characteristic: an overwhelming interest in expressing the secretly endured loneliness, passion, desire, and pain of love. The poets seem hardly concerned at all with creating any objectified image of the men or women they love.

Japanese love poetry, in other words, offers only an elusive image of the person to whom the poem is dedicated, an image virtually merged with the background. The center of the poem is not the object of the poet's love, but the poet's lament over that love, which pours forth like smoke from an active volcano. Japanese love poems, for the most part, are laments for an unrequited love.

It might be argued that love songs in general are laments for disappointed love. Even the Sebastatsi poem can be seen as an anguished cry for an unattainable love. But his verse is also filled with the image of woman as sacred, elevated beyond the poet's grief.

By contrast, we might say, Japanese love poetry is characteristically self-centered. Here poets lose themselves in their own inner world, among worries and solitude so extreme that even the presence of their lovers makes itself felt through sorrow and pain. The reader rarely sees a clear image of the other person because the relationship between two lovers is presented only so far as it affects the poet's own crucial interests.

Realism, of course, is out of the question in this situation. This is the basis for the highly refined expression of delicate and minute shades of emotion in Japanese poetry.

Here also is the reason for the rise and phenomenal flourishing of romantic stories and historical tales during the Heian period. A group of writers appeared who, though deeply rooted in the world of *waka*, could not contain themselves within its self-centered lyrical view of the world.

THE CHILL OF SLEEPING ALONE

Love poetry grows out of relationships between men and women in a particular society. In many Japanese love poems the loved one is treated not as a spiritual entity but as the object of sexual association, contact, and desertion. Countless beautifully worded verses on "love" prove to be astoundingly delicate verbal music on the chilling loneliness of being in bed alone.

> *Kaku to dani eyawa ibuki no sashimogusa*
> *sashimo shirajina moyuru omoi o*

> I wish I could just tell her
> of the love in my heart
> growing like moxa weed
> She does not know
> that I am burning for her
> like moxa from Mt. Ibuki

> Fujiwara Sanetaka

This poem from the *One Hundred Poems by One Hundred Poets* was originally in the section "Love" in Volume One of *Go Shui Waka Shu*. Its foreword reads: "sent to a woman for the first time." It simply says that no words could convey the extent of the poet's love -- but it does so in a highly contrived fashion, using devices found in many other poems. The meaning is "I couldn't possibly say that I yearn this much for her, although I really wish I could. I am like the moxa of the Ibuki region. Set on fire, I burn. I burn in my heart. But you will not see this fire in me. It is invisible."

The poet speaks single-mindedly of the pain he feels in love. His poem is centered on that theme. Here is another example, this time by Fujiwara Teika, editor of *One Hundred Poems by One Hundred Poets:*

> *Konu hito o matsuho no ura no yunagi ni*
> *yaku ya moshio no mi mo kogaretsutsu*

> Waiting for my love who will not come
> in the evening calm of Matsuho Bay
> where seaweed is being roasted for salt
> roasting like seaweed I yearn for him

This poem makes explicit reference to Kasa no Kanamura's poem in Man'yo Shu:

> *. . . Awajishima matsuho no ura no*
> *asanagi ni tamamo karitsutsu*
> *yunagi ni moshio yakitsutsu*
> *amaotome aritowa kikedo*
> *miniyukamu yoshinonakereba. . . .*

> . . . I've heard a maiden lives by the sea
> at Matsuho Bay
> at Awaji Island
> In the morning calm
> she hunts precious seaweed
> In the evening calm
> she roasts it for salt.
> I'd like to go see her
> But I have no means. . . .

Teika's poem refers to the extraction of salt from seaweed soaked in salt water. People gather seaweed, pile it on rocks, and pour sea water over it. Afterwards they roast the weed to crystallize the salt on its surface, then dissolve the impure salt in water, skim the mixture, and cook down the liquid to produce pure salt.

Composed in 1216 and included in the section "Love," its mood is quite different from that of Teika's usual mysteriously ornate poems. But he must have regarded it with particular pride, since as editor he chose it for inclusion in the *One Hundred Poems by One Hundred Poets*. It can be paraphrased as follows:

> Waiting for my love who does not come -- this is like being roasted.
> It is painfully, deadly calm -- there's not even a breeze. A man is

roasting seaweed. For the salt? What is roasting is, yes, myself.
Waiting for a man who will not come, yearning, pining after him,
tormenting myself.

The focus of the poem, the pain of waiting for a man who does not come, is
never explicitly stated. The persona of the poem simply presents her pain at
being slowly roasted in the fires of anxiety. Rhetorical devices -- related words,
double meanings -- evoke the scene, gently concealing the central theme of her
painful longing for and resentment toward this man. In the foreground we see
only a beautiful woman deep in thought, pensive and alone.

Against the evening calm of the ocean, where nothing else moves, smoke
rises slowly from the roasting seaweed. The fire is the woman's heart,
smoldering heavily in this symbolic setting. Her heart overflows with anxiety,
but her words are gentle and elegant. When the author chose this as
representative of his work, he must have had confidence in his delicate handling
of the entanglement of words and feelings.

Here again we have self-centered lament as the basic motif in a poem that
attempts to express the relationship between lovers. Highly elegant in manner,
this poem precisely crystallizes the cold loneliness of being in bed alone.

The same can be said of the following piece, ascribed to Kakinomoto no
Hitomaro:

> *Ashibiki no yamadori no o no shidario no*
> *naganagashi yo o hitori kamo nemu*

> Through the long night
> long as the trailing tail of
> a mountain pheasant
> must I sleep alone

Compare it with an anonymous poem from *Kokin Waka Shu*, (volume 14,
section 4: "Love"):

> *Samushiro ni koromo katashiki koyoi mo ya*
> *ware o matsuramu Uji no Hashihime*

> This evening too
> does a princess by the Uji River wait for me
> as she lies alone
> on just one robe
> spread over the woven straw mat

And the same stance is assumed in the following poem, which plainly refers to these last two:

> *Kirigirisu naku ya shimoyo no samushiro ni*
> *koromo katashiki hitori kamo nemu*

> Crickets chirp
> this cold frosty night
> I spread just one robe
> and sleep alone
> on a woven straw mat

Fujiwara Yoshitsune

This last poem uses a series of "s" and "k" sounds to emphasize the feeling of cold, while expressing inconsolable loneliness at sleeping in a solitary bed. "I spread just one robe" contrasts with the usual lovers' custom of lying on both their robes layered together.

   Sonorous and superb as this verse is, we should not lose sight of the fact that it is based on the two earlier poems just quoted. In fact, the line of influence goes back even farther, to an anonymous poem in *Man'yo Shu* (vol. 9) that is the basis for the *Kokin Waka Shu* poem "This evening, too. . . ."

> *Waga kouru imo wa awasazu tamanoura ni*
> *Koromo katashiki hitori kamo nemu*

> The love I yearn for
> will not see me
> in Tama no Ura
> I must spread just one robe
> and sleep alone

Such poems on "sleeping alone" make up a substantial Japanese literary tradition. They could only be written in an environment where this tradition not only exists but is taken seriously. Much later, in the Muromachi period (1338-1573), a popular song runs as follows:

> *Toga mo nai shakuhachi o*
> *makura ni katari to nageatetemo*
> *sabishiya hitorine*

> My bamboo flute is not to blame
> but I hurl it at my pillow with a clack
> How lonely it is to sleep alone
> > *Kangin Shu* (1518)

Thus the tradition persists.

Lonely laments about having to sleep alone definitely constitute the most representative genre of Japanese love poems. This is apparent to anyone who looks closely at poetry from our ancient, middle, or modern periods. In devoting themselves to this theme the poets treat the lover not as a spiritual being but more as an object of direct sexual contact or alienation.

Depending on the poet's distance from the lover, he or she may sing a lament on sleeping alone, or on the morning after, or on having to brood (*nagame*) in the long, steady rain (*nagame*).

Man'yo Shu (vol. 4, "Love" section) includes this poem Fujiwara no Maro sent to Otomo on Sakanoue no Iratsume, the *grande dame* of Man'yo poets:

> *Mushibusuma nagoya ga shita ni fuseredomo*
> *imo toshi neneba hada shi samushimo*

> I lie under
> a warm linen cover
> soft and comfortable
> yet my skin feels cold
> without you next to me

There is a similar poem by Sone no Yoshitada. Unique among the poets of the mid-Heian Period, Yoshitada had a fresh, highly original style, but he was not well established in the central circle during his lifetime. After his death, however, he was gradually recognized and his poetry was collected in several court-sponsored anthologies. This is from his own collection, *Poems of Sone no Yoshitada.*

> *Yo wa samumi yodoko wa usushi*
> *furusato no imo ga hadae wa imazo koishiki*

> The night is cold
> the bedding is thin
> now more than ever I miss
> the warm skin of
> my hometown love

This love poem is as direct as any of Fujiwara no Maro's.

Yoshitada wrote many others of the same tenor, but to a different tune. The best of his love songs may be this one from *One Hundred Poems by One Hundred Poets*:

> *Yura no to o wataru funabito kaji o tae*
> *yukue mo shiranu koi no michi kana*

> Like the boatman who lost his oars
> as he was crossing the Yura Straits
> I am at a loss
> as to which direction
> my love is leading me

LOVE SONGS FROM THE *MAN'YO SHU*

My theme has been that in Japanese poetry there are innumerable cases where beautifully expressed feelings of love, however elaborate and delicate the language, turn out on closer reading to be sensitive but single-minded laments on the cold loneliness of sleeping alone.

In this respect the poems of the Heian period show more refinement than those of the Nara period, but are far less direct and straightforward in style. This demonstrates how the manner of writing poetry corresponds to the way love life was conducted in a given time and place.

During the Heian period, particularly after the 10th century, the Fujiwara clan established itself at the top of the hierarchy of courtiers. The officials, the intellectuals of the time, were appointed solely on the basis of lineage and family connections.

Women of good family were offered to high officials in order to establish important family ties. These court ladies played a large role in the making of Heian culture. Love relations between a man and woman of intellect and culture were conducted only within the well-defined structures of this caste-oriented society. To be outside those boundaries was to be a social failure.

Within a society of fixed classes the emotional values in expressions of love are bound to be formulated in certain fixed modes. Thus the social structure is basic to the tradition of court-sponsored anthologies, beginning with *Kokin Waka Shu.* Most of the women poets who have left their names in these Imperial anthologies were female courtiers. In other words, dauntless matriarchs such as Otomo no Sakanoue no Iratsume, the Nara Period poet, do not appear in court-sponsored collections after *Kokin Waka Shu.*

Here are two examples of Iratsume's forthright style of address to a man.

> *Komu to iu mo konutoki aru o*
> *koji to iu o komu towa mataji koji to iu mono o*

> Even when you say you'll come
> you fail to come
> as you say you won't come
> there's no use waiting for you to come
> since you say you won't come

> *Chidori naku saho no kawato no se o hiromi*
> *uchihashi watasu na ga ku to omoeba*

> The stream is wide
> at the Saho rapids

> where plovers sing
> So I will place a board for you to cross
> since I expect you to come over

These poems, two of four written in response to the three Fujiwara no Maro poems quoted earlier (including "I lie under / a warm linen cover"), are illustrative of the love poems of the Man'yo period. In the first the poet is playing with sound patterns. This is part of the evidence by which she proves herself his equal even as she reproaches his negligence. The second poem achieves the same effect for the reader through her use of the second person pronoun *na*, which later came to be used to designate a person inferior to the speaker, or, when used by a man, to designate a woman.

As Iratsume's poems demonstrate, Man'yo love poems are more clearly individualistic than the court love poems written since *Kokin Waka Shu*. This is especially true in the work of women poets. Kasa no Iratsume, for example, left 29 poems in *Man'yo Shu*, the outcome of an unfortunate love affair with Otomo no Yakamochi, who preserved her fervent songs. From "Twenty-four poems sent to Otomo no Yakamochi," here are some samples :

> *Waga yado no yukagegusa no shiratsuyu no*
> *kenuga nimo to na omohoyuru kamo*

> In my residence
> white dew on the evening glories
> seems about to disappear
> I feel I might too
> as I yearn for you

> *Asagiri no obo ni aimishi hito yue ni*
> *inochi shinubeku koiwataru kamo*

> An encounter uncertain as the morning mist
> makes me long for you all the more
> I die of love

Ise no umi no iso mo todoro ni yosuru nami
kashikoki hito ni koiwatarukamo

Waves surge, roaring over the Sea of Ise
where the gods live
such awesome waves, awesome as you
I will love you forever

Aiomowanu hito o omou wa otera no
gaki no shirie ni nukazuku ga goto

To be in love with a man
who does not love me
is like prostrating myself
beneath the hungry demons at the great temple

These are all deservedly well known poems. They prove her gift beyond doubt. Kasa no Iratsume's love poems stand out from those of all the other woman poets of the Man'yo period.

IZUMI SHIKIBU

Two hundred years after Kasa no Iratsume, Izumi Shikibu writes:

Seko ga kite fushishi katawara samuki yo wa
waga tamakura o ware zo shite nuru

When I feel the night cold beside me
where once my love slept next to me
I pillow my head on my own arm
and sleep alone

Tsurezure to sora zo miraruru omouhito
amakudari komu mono nara nakuni

I find myself pondering
staring at the sky --
would that my love might
descend from the heavens

Kurokami no midare mo shirazu uchifuseba
mazu kakiyarishi hito zo koishiki

I long for you
You smoothed my hair first
when I lay down
oblivious to my black hair
falling unkempt

Sutehatemu to omou sae koso kanashikere
kimi ni narenishi waga mi to omoeba

It is sad even to think
of casting off this mortal body
because it is so used to being with you

Hakanashi to masashiku mitsuru yume no yo o
odorokade nuru ware wa hito kawa

A life passed away
before my very eyes
Knowing this is a world of dreams
I sleep on without surprise
Am I human?

Mono omoeba sawa no hotaru mo waga mi yori
akugare izuru tama ka tozo miru

As I am deep in thoughts of love
a firefly floats up above a stream

> Is it my soul
> lured out of me, yearning?

Izumi Shikibu was a woman of rare temperament, brimming with immense and self-centered energy. In poems like "When I feel the night cold beside me," "I long for you," or "It is sad even to think," this tempestuous energy brings new life to the tradition of love expressed through a poetry of physical contact. Izumi Shikibu was a genius who could turn physical sensation into the loftiest poetic sublimation.

Perhaps it was the same genius that gave her poems a frequent philosophical turn. "A life passed away / before my very eyes," probably written when she had lost her lover and was living in a daze, shows her finally looking at reality directly and objectively. "Suddenly the death of my love forced me to realize the mutability of life. Day in and day out I live in a stupor. Yet without any surprise at the evanescence of this dream world I sleep night after night as I did before. Am I human?" The psychology is complex. Izumi Shikibu's special gift lay in condensing such perplexed sentiments into a single breath.

She sent the following poem to a man with whom she was briefly involved.

> *Shiratsuyu mo yume mo konoyo mo maboroshi mo*
> *tatoete ieba hisashikarikeri*

> White dews
> dreams
> this life
> and phantoms --
> they all seem eternal
> after this.

Dews, dreams, this life, phantoms -- all are made into metaphors of mutability. But compared to the lovers' brief encounter, these all seem "eternal." The boldness of the expression "they all seem eternal/ after this" makes her very unlike her Heian contemporaries. Only a woman who dedicated herself to love could be so decisive.

Chapter Three

HEART AND WORDS

Medieval Japanese poetics and art theory are now often discussed in terms of "symbolism." That term, of course, is never actually used in medieval essays, and the practices it indicates do not correspond very closely to those of the French Symbolist movement of the late 19th century. The French movement had a clear program, defined in Jean Moréas' confident symbolist manifesto of 1886, while "symbolism" as applied to medieval Japanese poetry is a broad, metaphorical, rather vague term.

But the term is a useful one. If we leave technical definitions aside, both the central concept and the historical development of medieval *waka* display strong elements of symbolism. A brief look at the Japanese view of late 19th century French Symbolism will help clarify the point. Terada Toru touches upon the "cosmic nature" of the work of the best Symbolists:

> Mallarmé is not alone in his idealistic tendencies. He deeply sympathized with the sublime novelist, Villiers de l'Isle Adam, in his detestation of science and pragmatism. In Mallarmé this crystallized into a belief that "all this world's existence will complete itself in a copy of a book." Poetry, as an allusion to ideas, should be equal to the world. Hence his pure but simultaneously ambiguous vision, captured, one could say, on the shore of a vast nothingness. To write such poems poets must desert the world, become ascetic, and live their beliefs, so to speak. Mysticism, a common factor in all Symbolists, inevitably arises from this attitude. On the other hand, this lonely, quiet, pure existence can bring about a poetic adventure that is both bold and absolutely progressive. As the flux of consciousness and its delicate inner movements are consciously perceived, traditional verse forms must undergo reorganization and

a revitalization from within. Not only that, but things must be given names free of all worldly entanglements, so that the most innocent and vivid image of the object can be evoked. Poetry must exist, not as a description or a report, but as the bearer of news from the conceptual world.

*The Shincho Concise Dictionary
of World Literature*, Section II

I quote this passage to show how Mallarmé's poetics, at least as manifested in its purest form, has strong similarities with the poetics of medieval Japanese poetry. When we Japanese think of poets who "desert the world, become ascetic, and live their beliefs, so to speak," we instantly recall Shunzei, Teika, and Saigyo, and, from a later period, Shinkei, whose theory on linked verse seems to correspond with the esthetics of the Noh masters Zeami and Zenchiku. And finally we think of the great *haikai* poet Basho who actually lived these words. This is the reason that symbolism is so often mentioned in connection with the poetry of medieval Japan.

Does medieval *waka* possess a "cosmic nature?" To offer an answer without defining what constitutes "cosmic nature" may be begging the question. Still, I feel justified in saying that medieval *waka* is lacking in that particular characteristic. Or rather, that it seldom even brings this idea to consciousness.

Terada shares the grounds for his recognition of this quality in Mallarmé with Paul Valery, who spoke of "the strictness of [Mallarmé's] methodology, as demonstrated by his firm position on giving equal treatment to a sequence of matters ranging from the minuscule to the gigantic." Mallarmé's rejection of a rigid poetics, arbitrarily applied to every work, raises his approach to the level of an inner algebra, penetrating and grasping the essence of poetry. To me *waka* shows no such strict methodology.

We might be tempted to take this absence of methodology for granted. After all, the poetics of *waka* was formulated long before that of Mallarmé. But I think the difference is more than a function of historical time. The ideology behind *waka* simply lacks the so-called "inner algebra" to make any discussion of a "cosmic nature" useful.

In spite of all the similarities and differences between *waka* and French symbolism, there does exist in medieval Japanese poetry a "mysticism" which constitutes an "allusion to ideas." Most of the "symbolist" concerns of Japanese poetry in the medieval era are embodied in one word: *yugen*.

Yugen certainly leads one to a "mystic nature." But it does not carry the weight of any cosmic nature that can be compared to "an inner algebra" -- even taking into account the influence of Buddhist philosophy. Though Tendai Buddhism, based on the Lotus Sutra, deeply affected poetics from Shunzei to Shinkei, the cosmic principle of Buddhism lies strictly outside of poetry. And poetry itself, or poetics itself, is not necessarily cosmic in nature.

THE CONCEPT OF *YUGEN*

The concept of *yugen* has penetrated into the essence of medieval Japanese poetics and general art theory. One of the many excellent discussions of this phenomenon, the now classic text *On Yugen* by Nossé Asaji, begins by discussing the special nature of the word.

Nossé points out that this word was originally used in Chinese philosophical terminology to indicate something "profound and unfathomable, therefore not easily penetrated by the human mind." But when the word came to Japan it was used to express "artistic excellence" in Chinese style poetry, *waka*, music, linked poetry, and Noh drama. He continues:

> From the point of view of the pursuit of beauty, this word has some interesting characteristics. It is a fact that it generally indicates the depth or height of beauty rather than its nature or color.
>
> This word indicates the endlessly expanding beauty of suggestiveness, the beauty of profundity that goes ever deeper. What this beauty contains is a "vast nothingness." Therefore it can hold within itself all that *awaré* [noble pathos] can achieve at its highest, everything that *en* [sensuality] shows at its best, whatever *sabi* [elegant simplicity] can hold at its deepest, and all that *yu* [grace] contains at its most refined. It also accommodates any or all of these combined in a delicate balance.

This is truly an interesting observation. *Yugen* is referred to as indicating the "height or depth of beauty," rather than the "nature or color of beauty." This attitude is also characteristic of the style *ushin*, praised so highly by Teika, and it governs the concepts *karabiru* (dry), *kareru* (spare), *hieru* (crystalline), *yaseru* (lean), and *samushi* (icy), the words Shinkei preferred in denoting superb beauty.

All of these concepts grew from the basic ground of *yugen*. But all changed in implication, moving from the *yugen* connotation of gentle sensory attractiveness to one of a beauty more cold and severe. And again, all the concepts, including that of *yugen*, refer to a state of mind for which there exists no definite, objective measure. Nossé's comment on the "height or depth of beauty" as opposed to its "nature or color" points precisely to this subjective quality.

It may be possible to find some objective standard of judgment for the "nature and color of beauty." These qualities deal with a measurable realm of beauty, and we could use any of several convenient methods, such as categorizing, measurement, and comparative observation to form a judgment. But once we talk about the height or depth of beauty, we are driven into a realm where convenient forms of measurement do not exist. There is simply no objective gauge for determining the "depth" or "height" of beauty.

So one naturally turns to the depth or height of one's own mind. Depending on the expanse of our minds, the beauty facing us can be deep or shallow. Apply this approach to our five senses and we find that the concepts of *yugen* and the rest are liveliest when linked with senses for which there is no gauge -- touch, smell, and taste -- and least alive when applied to sight or hearing, senses which, by comparison, are measurable.

HEART AND WORDS

Shinkei reportedly said once that "linked poetry should be withered and cold" (*Yamanoue Soji Ki*, The Way of the Tea Ceremony). He also said "Nothing is more lustrous than ice" (*Hitori Goto*). I take these statements to represent an extreme development of the concept of *yugen*. They do so by ascribing elegant and profound sensory qualities to experiences that seem totally opposed to *yu-en*, the idea of gentle sensory attractiveness within the concept of *yugen*. But it is noteworthy and distinctive that these statements ultimately relate to the sense of touch, such as the coldness of ice. They exclude all visual elements -- floweriness, brilliance, clarity of outline or color. It seems some mad fever of subjectivity drives both the artist and his readers to greater "depths" or "heights."

Why is this so? Here we have the issue of "heart" and "words."

The editors of *Man'yo Shu* demonstrated their awareness of the many ways there are to express "heart" when they created such categories as "Direct Expressions of the Core of the Heart," "Thought Likened to Things," "Allegorical Songs," and so forth. Ki no Tsurayuki later took up the issue in his native-script preface to *Kokin Waka Shu*, saying "Japanese poetry is leaves of words sprouted from the seed of man's heart." In this formulation the "heart," the seed from which grow the leaves of words, is the source of poetry.

The ancient poets of Japan had one thought in common: the ideal may be a total fusion of heart and words, but if one is forced to make a choice, "heart" comes first. Fujiwara Teika says:

> My late father (Shunzei) used to say that we should choose words that have their source in our hearts. One person has likened this matter of poetry to flowers and seed, saying that the ancient songs all had the seed, but neglected the flowers, while recent poetry minds only the flowers, but pays no attention to the seed. I certainly agree with him. The preface to *Kokin Waka Shu* says this, too. . . . The seed here is heart; the flowers, words.
>
> *Maigetsusho*

Teika is here talking about the process of writing poetry. But he applies this same standard to the process of selecting superb poetry:

> First of all, the heart must be deep, its height tall and tactful, overflowing beyond words, noble in figure. The words are linked in the most unusual fashion, yet smooth and pleasing to the ear. Faint images unusual in appearance will arise. The overall mood is such that the mind does not rest. This is poetry.
>
> *Maigetsusho*

The "heart," then, must be "deep." When the heart is deep it flows "beyond words." From this point symbolism and a symbolic nature inevitably developed in the poetry of medieval Japan.

Because it is difficult to conceptualize "heart" as Teika uses the term, it is often discussed by analogy, by inference from an inner sensory touch. If we force a concept on it, starting in ancient times we come upon ideas like "clear" and "clean." This concept extends from the clean "white" of primitive conditions to the desolate, colorless, transparent state of mind that follows the denial of all color.

There is no need to bring up ancient purification rites to illustrate the Japanese sense of cleanliness. Sei Shonagon, for example, gives us this list of "elegant and noble" things: "Sweetened shaved ice in a new metal bowl. A crystal rosary. Wisteria blossoms. *Ume* flowers with the snow falling on them." (*Makura no Soshi*, #42)

Likewise, in *The Tale of Genji* Murasaki Shikibu has the Shining Prince say,

> Rather than cherry blossoms in their prime, or even autumnal leaves, it is certainly the clear winter sky with the moon and the snow reflecting each other that is unearthly. Even though it does not have colors, it appeals to our hearts. It makes us think of matters beyond this world. The pleasure and pathos of things both abound. Only a thoughtless person would call this an example of something uninteresting.
>
> > "*Asagao*"

Sei Shonagon may have been the "thoughtless" object of Murasaki's ridicule here, but she did make that sharp observation on recognizing a higher level of beauty in the incidence of white on white, or white inside white. Her refined sense of beauty certainly deserves respect.

If we suddenly leap forward into the modern period, we find in Mori Ogai's *Uta Nikki* (Song Diary) this piece on the ideal *waka*:

> *Uta mo kakare koori o moreru hari no ban,*
> *hogara ni sukite mienu kumanaki*

> Let a poem be
> a crystal bowl filled with ice

> so clear and transparent
> the farthest corner can be seen.

Here too we see adoration and praise for a world of clarity that points to colorlessness.

To sum up, the *waka* of medieval Japan displays a "symbolism" that was decidedly mystic, single-mindedly pursued purity, and produced many "ascetics." But it was somewhat different from French symbolism, described by Terada as having "strictness, methodology, and an established viewpoint enabling one to give equal treatment to a series of matters ranging from the minuscule to the gigantic." In Japan that sort of concern was left instead to religious philosophy, such as propounded in *Shobo Genzo* by the priest Dogen. Poets, on the other hand, pursued the realm of the profound and transcendent -- *yugen* in its original sense -- through an extreme refinement of the senses, in an effort to divorce themselves from colors, in effect to transcend colors.

COURT-SPONSORED POETRY

There was a genuine deepening and purifying of esthetic values during the period we call the middle ages, in a process that is relevant to our literary life even now. But what sort of social and literary environment produced it?

There are many clues, many avenues of investigation to follow. I would like to look at the subject from the perspective of the changes in court-sponsored anthologies of poetry between the Heian and the Kamakura periods, and compare the *Kokin Waka Shu*, which appeared in 905, at the prime of the Heian period, to the *Shin Kokin Waka Shu*, which dates from 1205, the beginning of the middle ages.

We have noted that court-sponsored anthologies were collections of the "best" older and contemporary poems, chosen by authoritative editors working under imperial decree. As the making of *Kokin Waka Shu* clearly shows, these imperial selections were compiled with the intention of praising the virtues of the emperor, celebrating the peacefulness of his reign, and building him a monument of poems that conveyed the essence of Japanese culture. The poems selected for inclusion in these compilations were affirmations of this world, celebrating its peace and glorifying the present. Their dominant esthetic principles were elegance and beauty.

The esthetic standards were those of the courtiers. For these insiders, and for those whom they influenced, these standards seemed so self-evident that no one even dreamed of questioning them. Here, for example, we have a verse by Tsurayuki from *Kokin Waka Shu* "composed upon visiting a mountain temple."

> *Yadori shite haru no yamabe ni netaru yo wa*
> *yume no uchi nimo hana zo chirikeru.*

> As I sojourned overnight
> in the mountain village in Spring —
> cherry blossoms cascading
> even in my dreams
>
> Vol. 2: "Spring"

The universal esthetic sense of this verse makes it easily understood even by those who have never visited a mountain temple. The season is Spring. The place is a temple in the valley. There is an overnight sojourner. This much alone should call up esthetic sensations for courtiers in the capital. In Tsurayuki's time a visit to a temple in the country or the mountains was not a serious religious act, nor were out-of-town excursions necessarily impelled by worldly worries. An excursion was a way of pursuing beauty and elegance.

Young Tsurayuki could not have been remote from the mood of flowery lasciviousness, from the hedonistic and idyllic life of his fellow courtiers, when he wrote this verse during the Kanpyo and Engi periods (c890-920). He sang of cherry blossoms cascading on a Spring night at a mountain temple. The image of cascading petals in this verse would have been accepted with complete sympathy by many. It was not just a description of Tsurayuki's personal experience on a given day -- it was an image that would be appreciated as the embodiment of the esthetic mood of his time.

In other words Tsurayuki -- and all the first-rate poets of the *Kokin Waka Shu* era -- aimed at a poetry in which a personal esthetic experience was shared with the whole of court society. These poets trusted so deeply in the power of their common experience that they believed the aim of a shared esthetic was attainable.

All the *Kokin Waka Shu* poems, whether selected by the editors or by others, have an air of happiness in this shared sensibility. Though the association might seem fantastic, *Kokin Waka Shu* as a whole reminds me of the Archaic Smile that characterizes early Greek sculpture. This quality is especially remarkable when we contrast *Kokin Waka Shu* poems with poems from *Shin Kokin Waka Shu*.

For purposes of comparison, here is a verse by Princess Shikishi (died 1201) from *Shin Kokin Waka Shu* on "recalling those days as vestal virgin."

> *Hototogisu sono kamiyama no tabimakura*
> *hono kataraishi sora zo wasurenu*

> Cuckoo!
> that time when I sojourned
> at the divine mountain
> you called to me faintly
> from the sky, which I can never forget
>
> Vol. 16: "Miscellaneous"

This poem is perhaps Shikishi's best; it is certainly one of her best known. "At the divine mountain" refers to the period when she was vestal virgin to the Kamo Shrine, from the first year of Heiji to the first year of Kao (1159-1169). The word *kami* means both "that time" and "divine" as applied to the mountain, that is, to the Kamo shrine. "That time" alludes to the practice of having the shrine princess stay overnight in the holy hall of the divine mountain during the April Kamo festival.

The cuckoo calls "faintly." It is April, after all. So, appropriately, the verse signifies "Oh cuckoo, I cannot forget the sky from which you faintly called over my pillow during my evening's sojourn in the holy hall of the divine mountain, during that Kamo festival."

But anyone who reads the poem aloud must sense that it expresses more than recollection or nostalgia about a particular sky from which a cuckoo's soft call came at a particular time. Isn't there another emotion intruding here? Doesn't it recall a secretly endured love for a man she met only briefly one mysterious night?

A Japanese reader can easily call up such associations as he croons the verse to himself. His mind is drawn to the limitless sky from which a cuckoo faintly calls, and he feels pathos.

This poem illustrates the concept of *yugen*. Yet I hesitate to call it elegant and sensual. Tsurayuki's verse on excursions was meant to appeal to courtiers through a shared esthetic. In that sense it was perfect of its type. Shikishi's poem tries to go deeper and deeper into the world of what is seen and heard.

There is no longer the extroverted happiness of the *Kokin Waka Shu* poet, who could assume a certain common ground with his audience on matters of life and esthetic sensibility. Where Tsurayuki could emphasize common experience, turning it into communal pleasure, Shikishi writes a melancholy monologue, concentrating the mind's eye on the eternally intangible.

As a rule Shikishi's poems neither address others nor invite us to share in the joy of living. This trend is characteristic of the poetry of the middle ages in general, and is the essence of *Shin Kokin Waka Shu*. Verse had come to pursue "faintness" or "darkness," and especially "depth," rather than "scope" or "richness."

CHANGES IN COURT-SPONSORED POETRY

The essence of court-sponsored anthologies remained praise of imperial virtue, celebration of the peaceful life, and the erection of a monument to the cultural heritage of past and present. However, the 300 years between *Kokin Waka Shu* and *Shin Kokin Waka Shu* saw substantial changes in how these principles were applied. A basic tenet of *Kokin Waka Shu* was the affirmation of reality and the enjoyment and glorification of the present. At the risk of oversimplification, we can say that by contrast *Shin Kokin Waka Shu* tends more toward world-weariness, toward a barren view of life.

Even *Shin Kokin Waka Shu* poems that treat the seasons display a deep and characteristic feeling for the inconstancy of life. That is precisely the source of the collection's charm. Here, for example, is another poem by Princess Shikishi.

> *Ato mo naki niwa no asaji ni musubohore*
> *tsuyu no sokonaru matsumushi no koe*

> My yard is rank with weeds
> where no footsteps are heard
> Trapped in the weeds

under the dew

a cricket cries

Vol. 5: "Autumn"

"Where no footsteps are heard" conveys complete absence, complete desertion. "Rank with weeds" indicates a lack of care, and "*musubohore*," or "trapped," though it refers directly to the cricket, also describes the person in the deserted, ramshackle house. She has seen no visitors and is full of sorrow and loneliness.

Then the word *musubohore* prompts "dew." The cricket is not simply hiding within scattered weeds, it is closed in by the cold dew collected on them. Incidentally, though we normally think of dew forming on the tips of leaves, once the cricket is presented as crying from "under the dew" we get an impression of dew collected heavily from leaf-tip to root. All of these effects give the poem a psychological plane above the level of a simple description of weeds, dew, and cricket.

There was good reason for this. In the Heian literary tradition "dew" instantly suggested "tears," and a cricket singing from "under the dew" cannot help evoking the image of a person who, unknown to others, is drenched in tears. The person is a woman, of course. The cricket (*matsu mushi*) is verbally associated with the verb "to wait" (*matsu*). Since marriage at that time consisted of visits to the woman by the man, the one who waited had to be a woman.

So this poem, appearing in the "Autumn" section of *Shin Kokin Waka Shu*, is also a song of love's lament. Readers of the time would appreciate its sorrow, and would feel its sensuality and pathos.

It is true that this particular poem was written on an assigned theme. But because its author is Princess Shikishi, a noblewoman whose life was full of misery, as a modern reader I cannot help sensing in it her personal view of life, if not her own experience.

THE EMBODIED CONSCIOUSNESS OF HER TIME

When she served as shrine maiden at the Kamo Shrine Shikishi was princess to ex-Emperor Goshirakawa. But the strongest memories of her life would have come from watching her uncle, ex-Emperor Sutoku, her brother, Prince Mochihito, and her nephew, Emperor Antoku, thrown into battle and destroyed in the relentless chain of events that led to the collapse of their aristocratic regime.

Her mood of painful sorrow is evidenced by the texture of her expression of her feelings, so fully developed that it is worth discussing on a technical basis. Shikishi's special point of view was strong enough to assert itself even in poems composed to assigned themes. I will quote a few here.

> *Nokori naku ariake no tsuki no moru kage ni*
> *honobono otsuru hagakure no hana*

Bathed in the light of
the moon at dawn
petals faintly fall
hidden among leaves

> *Yugiri mo kokoro no soko ni musubitsutsu*
> *wagami hitotsu no aki zo fukeyuku*

Evening·mist also curls
at the bottom of my heart
I am alone
as the autumn deepens

> *Mishi koto mo minu yukusue mo karisome no*
> *makura ni ukabu maboroshi no uchi*

What I have seen
what I have yet to see
are ephemera that float
above my pillow
in fleeting sleep

> *Kururu ma mo matsubeki yo kawa*
> *adashino no sueha no tsuyu ni arashi tatsu nari*

Are we spared even for a brief moment
while the sun sets?
A storm rises over the dew on the tips of leaves
in Adashino, the burial grounds

Hito shirezu mono omou sode ni kurabebaya
michikuru shio no nami no shitakusa

Unknown to him, I pine for him
and cry into my sleeves
drenched like weeds
under the waves
as the tide comes in

As Shikishi tries to capture objects which are simultaneously true to her inner reality and to the standard poetic conventions of her age, she is strongly attracted to sharp, narrow segments of experience, to dark areas deeply buried, or to places filled with dream phantoms.

For example, Shikishi talks of the softly falling flowers in the faint moonlight of a Spring daybreak. But the flowers she observes are not in plain view. She does not say "petals fall." She says petals fall "hidden among leaves." The verse takes on an extra dimension from the flashes of her wavering mind, a scope far beyond the simple presentation of scenery.

The reader is compelled to look into Shikishi's eyes, which seem singularly focused on the place hidden by the leaves. At this point the reader begins to wonder if the falling flower behind the leaves might be an image of the poet herself, as she sees herself in her daydreams.

Her unique grasp of objects is evident in the verses quoted above. She favors unusual angles on objects -- their inside, edge, or back -- rather than clear frontal views. This characteristic posture is a manifestation of Shikishi's personality. The verse we have considered at some length, "My yard is rank with weeds / where no footsteps are heard / Trapped in the weeds / under the dew / a cricket cries" crystallizes her sensitivity in viewpoint and language.

A WAY OF SEEING

By any objective standard Princess Shikishi had high noble standing. Even in those times of drastic social change it would have been possible for her to live at court in self-satisfied silence. There was still room for such happiness, even under a dying regime, but she never stopped casting her eyes toward the darkest, faintest aspects of worldly phenomena, as if she were a woman somehow trapped by a fatal attraction to all things fearsome and ominous. Her obsession with such matters, especially given her position and rank in society, offers eloquent proof that she was a poet of special character.

Her verse expresses in purest form the views and feelings of an aristocracy facing its destruction in the transition from ancient times to the middle ages.

As we consider the development of poetry in medieval Japan, seen clearly in the appearance of "symbolic" poetic techniques, this highly individual woman poet presents us a number of interesting issues. Her penchant for looking at "ends," or "inside" or "beneath" things, might correspond in ideological terms to milleniarism, a premonition of ultimate catastrophe. But what is most striking is how she crystallizes her insights into images.

Chapter Four

DEPTH, NOT KNOWLEDGE

The medieval period plays a central role in shaping Japanese ideas, art forms, and patterns of behavior. The assimilation of Buddhist principles helped make it the most contemplative of times. Its political turmoil made it the most active of times.

I have tried to show how medieval poetry contains this same combination of spiritual withdrawal from the world and personal involvement in its affairs. There is no poet more central, more important to this period than Fujiwara Shunzei, and none so truly representative of the character of the age.

Fujiwara Shunzei lived through the end of the Heian and the rise of the Kamakura periods. His poetry reflects the time in which he lived, yet his thought and his poetry penetrate beyond that range of experience.

SHUNZEI AND HIS TIME

Fujiwara Shunzei was born in 1114, during the reign of Emperor Toba. By the time he died at 91 in 1204, just three years after Princess Shikishi, he had lived through the reigns of nine more emperors: Sutoku, Konoe, Goshirakawa, Nijo, Rokujo, Takakura, Antoku, Gotoba, and Tsuchimikado.

The most respected of poets in the latter stages of his career, he remained an active writer and produced important work right to the end of his unusually long life.

Appointed by ex-Emperor Goshirakawa to edit the court-sponsored anthology *Senzai Waka Shu*, he completed it at age 74 in 1187, 282 years after Ki no Tsurayuki finished editing *Kokin Waka Shu*, the first court-sponsored anthology.

Senzai Waka Shu was to be the last anthology of the Heian period, as *Kokin Waka Shu* was the first. The work of the editors of the two collections, Tsurayuki and Shunzei, marked the beginning and the end of the Heian period in poetry, and strongly influenced later poetic theory and practice.

Shunzei lived through the decline of the Heian era, a period when the Buddhist concept of transiency -- the inevitable loss of all temporal riches -- was deeply felt. The warrior class, having realized its own strength during the Hogen battles (when Shunzei was 43) and the Heiji battles (when he was 46), quickly took control of all political power and completely shut out the court. After losing its struggle for political control to the more powerful warrior class, the court immersed itself in cultural concerns with a sense of urgency that we see in no other period. Former Emperor Gotoba, for example, devoted himself to poetry, as demonstrated in the compilation of the court-sponsored *Shin Kokin Waka Shu.*

Shunzei was 54 when Taira no Kiyomori became Prime Minister (*Dajo-Daijin*). He was 70 when the Taira clan was wiped out in the Juei Wars. The Minamoto clan took full control of power when he was 73, and a year later he completed *Senzai Waka Shu.*

He died one year after the last Minamoto ruler, Sanetomo, became shogun at the age of 12. By then political power was already shifting to the Hojo family.

Amid all these changes Shunzei's personal advancement came slowly. He was finally appointed to the third rank and joined the class of courtiers when he was 55. Between 59 and 63 he enjoyed the highest position he was to hold, that of *Kotaikogu Daibu*, or head of palace, for the empress-dowager, the biological mother of the then-current Emperor Takakura.

The uncertainty of life was certainly part of Shunzei's experience. When he was 64 he saw his son-in-law arrested for treason, exiled, and executed. In 1190, the first year of the Kenkyu reign, Shunzei, then 77, lost his friend, the poet Saigyo. By this time he himself was first among poets, in reputation and in practice, and served as judge in many poetry competitions.

In the eighth year of Kenkyu (1197), Shunzei, aged 84, wrote *Korai Futei Sho* (*Styles Ancient and Modern*) at the request of the Princess Shikishi. She had asked him "What does it mean to say a poem's form is good and its words are interesting?" In other words, he was asked to define the essence and characteristics of fine poetry. Stirred by the question, Shunzei returned an answer that disclosed the essence of his poetics, an answer memorable because it marks the beginning of medieval Japanese poetics.

SHUNZEI'S CHOICE

We will look at Shunzei's poetics after we look at his poetry. The following two pieces are probably his best known.

> *Yu sareba nobe no akikaze mi ni shimite*
> *uzura naku nari hukakusa no sato.*

> As evening comes
> autumn winds over the field
> chill me through
> quails call in this village of rank grass

> *Yo no naka yo michi koso nakere omoi iru*
> *yama no oku nimo shika zo nakunaru*

> Not a single right path in this world --
> as I enter the deep of the mountains
> pondering
> a deer calls

Shunzei included both poems in *Senzai Waka Shu*. The first he thought to be his best. The second was included in *One Hundred Poems by One Hundred Poets*. The editor, Shunzei's son Teika, obviously regarded it highly.

Kamo no Chomei's *Mumyo-sho* records an episode connected with the verse "As evening comes." It seems that the priest Shun-e, Chomei's poetry master, visited Shunzei and asked him what he thought was his best poem, mentioning that this piece had created quite a stir:

> *Omokage ni hana no sugata o sakidatete*
> *ikue koekinu mine no shirakumo*

> Sending visions of cherry blossoms ahead
> how many peaks did it cross to be here
> a white cloud over a mountain top

Shunzei disagreed, saying he considered "As evening comes" his finest work. Reporting this to Chomei, Shun-e suggested that "chill me through" is too explanatory, not quite suggestive enough.

This is a very interesting critique. Within its context "chill me through" certainly seems too explanatory. But I believe that Shunzei fully anticipated this criticism, yet still chose to use the expression. If I am correct, he may have had a premonition of the new shade of meaning that would soon attach itself to this word (*shimiru*).

In Chapter Two we examined the significance of the term *shimiru*, "to penetrate," in Japanese poetry. Here that term is translated with the sense "chill me through." In the middle ages this sensation was usually applied to a less simply sensory, more spiritual level of experience. It seems to me that the verse "As evening comes" consciously manifests this change.

As for the verse "Not a single right path in this world," its sense is as follows:

> Ah the vulgar world, there's no true path here. In this deep mountain where I've come with my thoughts a deer calls sadly. Is he calling for his wife? Is he recalling the sorrows of this world? The deer's call. . . .

It is clear that this verse states his desire for a secluded life and his sadness over the difficulty of attaining it.

In both poems the central figure is a solitary being. Both are quite removed from the splendor or sensuality that the term "aristocracy" normally evokes. At the center of each verse is a sense of the world's transiency.

THE SENSE OF TRANSIENCY

The sense of transiency is at the heart of medieval Japanese poetry. Let us observe it in concrete terms through a poem Shunzei composed as a young man. He prefaces it by saying, "In about the fifth year of Hoen (1139), when I, in mourning for my mother, was in retreat at Horinji temple, a storm raged through the night."

> *Ukiyo niwa ima wa arashi no yamakaze ni*
> *kore ya nareyuku hajime naruramu*

> The storm rages in this sorrowful world
> where I'd as soon be no more
> Might this be the beginning of
> growing used to this mountain storm

(This piece appears in "Sorrows," volume 8 of *Shin Kokin Waka Shu*, but I quote from his own collection, *Choshu Eiso*, because the preface there is more detailed.)

Shunzei's mother had died that year, when Shunzei was 26, and this poem grew out of his mourning. The word *arashi*, storm, also suggests *araji*, the desire for annihilation. So the poem suggests

> I no longer want to live in this world. As if showing an emotion of
> its own, the stormy wind blows down from the mountains. But I,
> mourning in the temple, tolerate that wind. It seems my heart grows
> accustomed to the wind, and to sorrow.

Shunzei had lost his father when he was only ten. His grief at the loss of his mother must have been deep. This may be why he was far more religious than his son Teika, and why he studied Buddhism so seriously. Even so this tone of resignation and self-examination at the age of 26 is notable. However the storm might rage, man does grow accustomed to it. He can even get used to the loss of his mother. That, he says, is the human condition.

Shunzei's sorrow is for the vanity of life, and at the same time for the nature of man, who becomes hardened even to his own lament. The sorrow in this poem is multifold, with the anguish of awakened consciousness as its basis. So at 26, already aware of conflicting selves within him, Shunzei is able to objectify and reconcile them in his poetry.

Here I think we can clearly see one phase of Japanese medievalism. Such an expression of the mind's multiple aspects is rarely found in *Kokin Waka Shu*, let alone in the even earlier *Man'yo Shu*.

When a poet, decrying the intransigence of life, focuses intently on the transiency and vanity of the world, attains full awareness of it, then writes about it, his poetry becomes self-reflective, contemplative, philosophical. At its deepest it also becomes ironic. Although we do not have many poems from Shunzei's twenties, what we do have exemplifies a creative process which, for me at least, testifies to his status as a true medieval poet.

The actual date from which to mark the start of the middle ages in Japan is a topic of some dispute. A commonly accepted boundary is the establishment of the Kamakura government (1192). By that time Shunzei was already in his late 70's. Psychologically, however, the medieval period actually began before that, as we see plainly in Shunzei's own poetics. He truly had the medieval consciousness of a man keenly aware of the conflicts among his own split selves and between himself and others.

That consciousness was not exclusive to poets in this most fervently religious and enthusiastic of times. In the tough, unyielding minds of leading Buddhists of the age a keen awareness of life's evanescence was matched with a steadfast urge to face reality. We might say that they brought a sense of life's fleeting nature to full awareness and began to overcome it within themselves. We find this medieval sense of the transiency of life not only in Shunzei but, later, in the essayist and poet Yoshida Kenko. Kenko is the author of the well-known collection of essays *Tsurezuregusa*, written early in the 14th century.

We might dub this process the expert objectification of self. It not only produces an awareness of one's own insignificance, it shows the way to an organized and detailed self-recognition, and to an awareness of the cold, objective truth surrounding the life of the self.

By objectifying the self one can finally achieve a vision of the invisible world. This discovery marks all of the first-rate minds of the medieval era.

TEIKA'S CRITIQUE OF TSURAYUKI

In 1209 Shunzei's son Teika sent his essay on poetry, *Kindai Shuka* (*Superior Poems of Our Time*), to Minamoto no Sanetomo. Its opening passage is famous:

Tsurayuki, in ancient times, preferred a style in which the conception of the poem was clever, the loftiness of tone difficult to achieve, the diction strong, and the effect pleasing and tasteful, but he did not compose in the style of overtones and ethereal beauty.

> *Fujiwara Teika's Superior Poems of Our Time*, trans. Robert H. Brower and Earl Miner (Stanford, California: Stanford University Press, 1967)

Teika here endorses his contemporaries, Minamoto no Tsunenobu and his son Toshiyori, and joins them in rejecting *Kokin Waka Shu* editor Tsurayuki and his followers. He also affirms the significance of the element of "overtones and ethereal beauty" for his time, as opposed to celebratory openness.

Teika's words "the conception of the poem was clever, the loftiness of tone difficult to achieve, the diction strong, and the effect pleasing and tasteful" are a good characterization of the Chinese-style poetry of the early Heian period -- and of the Tsurayuki-style Japanese poetry that, at its best, boasted of Imperial virtue and elegant feasting. Teika's insight was a painful awareness that such public poetry, poetry that seems to make a show of itself even in its elegant sensuality, was no longer possible for his generation. He clearly conceived of his suggestive, ethereal sensuality in opposition to such openly festive verse.

True, Tsurayuki and Teika do meet on the basic ground of preferring "heart" to "words." In Japanese poetics this was consistently the main topic of discussion. But on every other point they reveal a total divergence of ideals, clearly showing the difference between Teika's time and Tsurayuki's. Teika unquestionably felt that "clever, lofty, pleasing, and tasteful" poetry could be neither written nor read by his contemporaries without deep feelings of incongruity and emptiness.

This change in poetic ideals neatly distinguishes the full crest of court life (ca. 890-910) from its ebb. Tsurayuki could share his poetry with other courtiers in the firm belief that the esthetic it reflected was their common property. He could function as a poet by upholding a universally accepted poetic quality. The vast amount of poetry composed to be written on decorative screens (*byobu*), for instance, needed some social and esthetic framework to support it.

Teika, on the other hand, could not believe in any universal or shared communal view of poetry. With the pressures of the changing times in undeniable evidence, he felt the ground of court culture giving way beneath his very feet. His firm social foundation gone, the only choice was to cling all the more to his own view of poetry. So while Princess Shikishi could artlessly express her inner urges, Teika seriously and self-consciously expressed himself through ethereal sensuality and from multiple angles of view.

TEIKA'S COMMENT ON SHUNZEI

Teika's *Kindai Shuka* also contains an interesting passage about his father, Shunzei, that throws another striking sidelight on the issues of Teika's poetry. Teika reminisces to Sanetomo:

> For my part, I fully realize that I ought to have a thorough knowledge of poetry, whereas I have merely inherited the fame of two generations. At times I have been treated with honor, at times been spoken of with scorn, but lacking sufficient devotion to this art from the very beginning, I have learned nothing except how to put together a few odds and ends that people have refused to accept as poetry. Although my father's only instructions to me were the simple words, "Poetry is not an art which can be learned by looking afield or hearing afar; it is something that proceeds from the heart and is understood in the self," I never even groped my way far enough to experience the truth of what he said.
>
> *Fujiwara Teika's Superior Poems of Our Time*, trans. Brower and Miner

This passage is rife with the usual Japanese self-abasement, of course, but it is typical of Teika to say "I have learned nothing except how to put together a few odds and ends that people have refused to accept as poetry."

Even more noteworthy is his recording of his father's words on what poetry is and is not, the explicit expression of Shunzei's position and intent. Shunzei reveals a poignant insight into the reality of his times: though a residual glow of court culture was still in the air, an age had arrived when just "looking afield and listening afar" was not enough to write even a simple poem.

Previously, during the times of Ki no Tsurayuki and Fujiwara Kinto, poetry had been based on learning and a broad knowledge of custom. Fujiwara Kinto (966-1041) typifies poets of that age. He was a leading poet and theoretician of the mid-Heian period whom his contemporary Murasaki Shikibu described in her diary as an awesomely accomplished man of letters. His multi-faceted cultural refinement and wisdom, including talent in poetry and music, gave him high standing in a court where poetry was always part of the environment.

Shunzei did not deny the significance of cultural breadth. But at the same time he knew that in his era the pursuit of culture as such was no longer possible -- or rather no longer feasible. His awareness led to his assertion that "poetry is not an art which can be learned by looking afield or hearing afar. It is something that proceeds from the heart and is understood in the self." He handed down this attitude to his son Teika, who in actuality not only worked extremely hard at his art, but was probably superior to all other poets in "looking afield and listening afar" as well.

SHUNZEI'S POETICS

Sophisticated lyricism, the fundamental ideal of Heian poetry, was a part of Shunzei's inheritance. But what was commonly accepted as "lyricism" during the *Kokin Waka Shu* period came to seem gaudy and frivolous to his contemporaries. His poetics addresses this issue.

Shunzei's representative work on poetics is *Korai Futei Sho* (*Styles Ancient and Modern*). Written at the request of Princess Shikishi, it expressed his long-held convictions on poetry. Shunzei's views on the qualities of superior poetry are contained in its opening section:

> Lord Kinto, identifying the good of poetry, called it "Golden Jewels," and Michitoshi's preface to *Go Shui Waka Shu* contains such phrases as "words are like tapestries and the heart is deeper than the ocean." But poetry does not necessarily have to be a silken

tapestry. Some poems are simply read aloud or recited to somehow sound lyrical and pathos-filled. During recital the voice can make a piece sound better or worse than it is.

Lord Kinto's *Golden Jewels* is a collection of 78 poems ranging from post-*Man'yo Shu* times to his own era. Shunzei here subtly censures the style of the two collections of poetry he mentions, and by extension all of Heian literature, of which they are prime representatives.

At that time it was quite common to read poetry out loud or intone it in formal recitation for judging. Shunzei had ample experience with this practice as the most authoritative presence at court "poetry contests." His use of the word "somehow" is worth noting, for he is proclaiming that there is really no clear basis for value judgments or objective principles in appraising poetry.

Then where is there a basis for judgment? It lies beyond what can be physically determined or objectively explained. It lies in the heart. Shunzei's words to Teika -- "Poetry is not an art which can be learned by looking afield or hearing afar. It is something that proceeds from the heart and is understood in the self" -- and his assertion in *Korai Futei Sho* (*Styles Ancient and Modern*) both say exactly the same thing. His stance on this point is firm and consistent.

He presents this idea vividly in the opening section of *Korai Futei Sho*:

> As the renowned preface to *Kokin Waka Shu* says, poetry is leaves of words sprouted from the seed in man's heart. So if we visit flowers in Spring or view leaves in autumn without poetry, no one would know their colors or fragrances, and there would be no heart or source for them. Because of this, generations of emperors preserved poetry, and many distinguished families compete in the enjoyment of it.

Kubota Utsubo (1877-1967), one of the greatest modern *tanka* poets and author of several remarkable books on classical Japanese poetry, has discussed the significance of this passage:

> His central conception is that "if we visit flowers in Spring or view leaves in autumn without poetry, no one would know their colors or fragrances." Spring flowers and autumn leaves represent nature.

They are nature itself. Color and fragrance are its beauty, the beauty of nature. He tells us that the beauty of nature cannot be understood without poetry, or that it does not exist without poetry. He presents this as a self-evident proposition.

Of course, it is not as if we have no explanation for the proposition. He quotes the preface to *Kokin Waka Shu*, but his interpretation is unique. The statement there that "poetry is leaves of words sprouted from the seeds in man's heart" simply says that poetry contains immense variety. Shunzei conceived of the "seed" as the universal source, making all of nature the product of the heart.

As one strongly influenced by Buddhism, he probably feels no need for an explanation here. But once he applies this conception directly to poetry and says that the beauty of nature, or its allure, is singularly the property of the heart, we have to accept his belief as something beyond logic and rationality. This view of nature as a sensory entity, and of its allure as coming from the heart, may not be original with Shunzei, but he was the first to conceptualize it and postulate it as a basis for poetics.

At the peak of the Heian period, when Kinto and the other major poets of *Go Shui Waka Shu* were still alive, sensory attractiveness existed in an objective fashion and had wide prevalence. What struck Shunzei as too alluring seemed perfectly natural to those earlier poets. Having lived through a time of decline, Shunzei could not but view sensory allure as ultimately subjective. It existed nowhere outside -- only in his heart. Therefore, it could not have a scope of its own. It could only extend in depth if one tried to develop it.

> "The Poetic Theory of Fujiwara Shunzei, Emphasizing *En* (*Allure*), *Yugen*, and *Honkatori*," *Collected Works of Kubota Utsubo*, Vol.10: "Theory in Classical Literature II."

An elegant allure, conceived as profound rather than extensive, is exactly the concept expressed by the word *yugen*. It is the central element in all Japanese arts and letters: Japanese poetry, Chinese-style poetry and prose, linked verse,

Noh music, traditional music. Shunzei was the poet who best embodied its emerging character.

As we have seen, the Chinese term *yugen* originally implied a deep and unfathomable realm not readily penetrated by human wisdom. Imported into Japan, it was elevated to the status of esthetic terminology, finally attaining its position as the definition of supreme esthetic beauty. This process is interesting in its own right, but it is more important to realize that at the crucial turning point in the term's literary significance stood Shunzei, the poet who embodied the medieval consciousness of poetry grasped in its depth rather than its breadth of scope.

To *Shin Kokin Waka Shu* poets sounding the depths was without question the basic thrust of poetry. This means that these poets possessed sensibilities of extraordinarily high refinement. During the *Kokin Waka Shu* era only that collection's editors and a few other poets understood "poetry as the expression of a certain concept." But by the *Shin Kokin Waka Shu* era of the middle ages, conceptual understanding was taken for granted as a prerequisite for all poets, anthologized or not.

There were several reasons for this shift in attitude. The psychological pressures being brought to bear on the aristocracy as a result of sociopolitical changes was one such reason. On a more mundane level, another undeniable reason was the role played by poetry contests in giving the idea widespread currency.

In the early stages poetry contests were little more than a social game involving simple skills, but a more literary poetry contest quickly flourished, coinciding with the rapid fall of the aristocracy. These later contests promoted the tendency to think about the true nature of poetry.

Opponents at a poetry contest were divided into two sides, left and right. The judge of the contest had to give clear reasons for preferring one verse to another or holding both equal. To fulfill his task he had to call upon his knowledge of poetic styles, poetic sins, classic resources, and so forth, to clarify what he thought poetry should be at that stage of its development.

The poets competing in these contests thus had to consider these issues quite seriously as well, and in becoming concerned with the question of what poetry should be they also became sensitive critics. Fujiwara Shunzei, ruler of the competitions, stood at their head. When he whispered "*yugen*" the term was not simply accepted, it was highly regarded.

Let me emphasize this crucial point. Shunzei, the presiding critic-scholar of the poetry contests, with 90 years of accumulated learning and wisdom to draw upon, taught his son Teika that

> Poetry is not an art which can be learned by looking afield or hearing afar; it is something that proceeds from the heart and is understood in the self.

Teika took his words to heart. In them lies the truth of medieval Japanese poetry.

Chapter Five

THE FLOWER IN *WAKA*

Earlier in our reading of Japanese classical poetry we saw that the era of the *Man'yo Shu* particularly favored *ume* (Japanese apricot) blossoms. The *ume* was imported from China, and this made it all the more fresh and attractive to people of the Nara Period. That it is so fragrant it can be located by its scent even in the dark of night stirred the poetic imagination. In the succeeding Heian Period, however, cherry blossoms, which were not popular in the Nara Period, captured so much attention that to most people the word for flower, *hana*, actually came to mean cherry blossom.

Hana is consistently the most used word in Japanese poetry, art, and theater. Japanese esthetics is often described in terms of *setsu*, *getsu*, *ka* (snow, moon, flower). *Ka* is the Chinese reading of *hana*. We talk about "the flower of a man's heart." The Noh master Zeami's book on the art of Noh, *Fushi Kaden*, mentions the word flower well over a hundred times. As a result, this book is popularly known as *Kaden-Sho* (*The Book of the Flower*).

In Noh *hana* is not an actual flower but an abstract concept; still, the concept was eventually applied to real flowers, and so books dealing with flower arranging are also called *Kaden-Sho*. The late Kanze Hisao, who tried to revive the true spirit of Noh master Zeami in our times, used the word *hana* in the title of his last book.

Obviously *hana*, "flower", is a very important concept in Japanese art and theater. And while *hana* does not mean simply cherry blossoms, we can safely treat the two as synonymous in the world of *waka*, especially during and after the Heian Period.

This tradition persisted through the *haikai-no-renga* or linked verse of the Edo Period. *Haikai* means laughter or mirth. Unlike the *renga* of the preceding Muromachi period, *haikai-no-renga* was loaded with the humor of the daily life of common people. Yet it also treated *hana*, represented by cherry blossoms, with great reverence. One requirement of this linked verse form was the mention of both the moon and flowers. Flowers, for example, had to appear twice in the 36 lines of the verse; the moon had to appear three times. By retaining the moon and flowers as important elements the poets paid tribute to tradition.

The *haiku* master Basho had great respect for people who talked about flowers as Zeami or Saigyo did, and thought that he and his followers should also strive to create a flower of their own. He was strongly interested in the word flower, in real cherry blossoms, and in everything cherry blossoms represented.

There is an historical progression to this concept. As we read the *waka* of *Man'yo Shu* we notice something interesting: the poets do not show much interest in how the flowers fall, but rather in how they proudly bloom. The Heian period, however, began to see the bloom as something doomed to fall. And in *Shin Kokin Waka Shu* the poets pay extraordinary attention to how the flower falls, as if to say that flowers bloom only for the sake of falling. This focus reflects the concept of the inconstancy of life.

To depict flowers at the height of radiance the Japanese concentrate on the moment of their fall; that is a central characteristic of Japanese poetry, and of Japanese esthetics in general. The underlying Japanese concept of flowers is that they must fall, and good poems on flowers are often those which show insight into the moment of the fall. There are some poems about luxuriating flowers, of course, but those on falling flowers are in the overwhelming majority. To sing of falling flowers is to sing of time passing. Flowers bud, grow, bloom to the full and fall away before we can draw a breath; after their prime the flowers, especially cherry blossoms, fall rapidly. And that, post-Heian poets thought, symbolized life.

Does that mean the poems are sad? Not necessarily. When we look through poems on how flowers fall they do not appear to be simply sad, or desperate, or world-weary; rather the poets merge their identities with the falling flowers and fade into the passage of time. Somehow they see beauty in transience, glory in the flower at the moment of its fall. The idea seems to be that in the beauty of that moment, when we have lived out our limited span, we can see a glorious vision of the beyond. Closely related to Buddhist thought, this belief clearly exists in the Heian Era, when Buddhism was an important influence.

As it was not native, Heian Buddhism was not yet prevalent among the commoners. It was almost the exclusive property of the aristocracy. By this I mean that the aristocrats studied Buddhism. They marveled at the various Buddhist ideas, were amazed by the theoretical structure, and were stimulated by Buddhist events and rituals throughout the year. Priests in elegant robes would walk in a row, scattering flowers, chanting sutras in beautiful voices, offering to the imagination a vision of the Pure Land in the midst of life.

Therefore to build a Buddhist temple only the highest level of technology was appropriate. The temples were not like those we see now, of dark natural wood; they were brightly painted, often orange-red or bright green. The priests' robes were also brightly colored, and certain colors designated specific ranks.

Mt. Hiei in Kyoto was the center of large-scale Buddhist functions. Aristocrats climbed to various temples there to join in rituals or participate in events. For Heian aristocrats such experiences were an important part of their daily life. Just climbing Mt. Hiei took considerable effort, and participating in Buddhist rites in this lofty, mysterious place was an experience quite removed from everyday affairs. After spending a few days listening to the priests' chants and inhaling the fragrant incense, they must have felt they were coming closer to the other world, far from the troubles of this one.

The *Hokkekyo* (the Saddharmapundarika sutra) was chanted at Mt. Hiei. Its imagery, primarily of the afterworld, is more literary than that of other Buddhist scriptures. As the aristocrats listened it created a glorious vision in their minds. And when they viewed the falling flowers they did not simply lament over the death of beauty, but foresaw an unimaginably beautiful existence awaiting them.

Heian Buddhism, so pleasing to the esthetic sense, had prepared the stage for such visions. The poems on flowers in *Kokin Waka Shu* and other collections reflect this esthetic concept.

THE FLOWER AS THE BASIS OF ZEAMI'S NOH THEORY

Kokin Waka Shu was compiled around the beginning of the 10th century. *Shin Kokin Waka Shu* was compiled 300 years later.

Three centuries is a long time. The Fujiwara family's supremacy in the Heian aristocracy was long gone. Warriors, originally the hired guards of the Heian aristocrats, had accumulated enough power to rule the country, at first in the remote regions, ultimately from the capital. The Heike (Taira Family) and Genji (Minamoto Family) warrior clans held power successively, beginning a long period of warrior supremacy. Over the course of 300 years those who sang the songs of the aristocrats saw the basis of their existence dissolve.

Buddhism also changed. Unlike the ostentatious, academic, systematic Buddhism of the Heian period, Kamakura period Buddhism addressed the common people. The priests Shinran and Nichiren, and even Dogen after his return from China, left the capital to go into outlying areas and make contact with commoners. Without this effort Buddhism in Japan would have perished. While these priests originally were influenced by the Buddhism of the capital, they became earthy practitioners rather than mere preachers of tenets they had learned from their predecessors.

Dogen of the Zen sect retained more of the academic stance than the others. But even Dogen rejected the capital's brand of Buddhism, which seemed to exist only for the sake of the aristocrats. Born to a courtier's family, Dogen was a member of the illustrious aristocracy. He took up the Buddhist way at an early age, went to China during the Sung Dynasty to study Zen, and returned home a Zen master.

Had he chosen to he could have lived out his life in gorgeous robes as a priest among the aristocrats. He dared, however, to decline the priest's robe offered him by the Emperor. Convinced that Buddhism would not survive without breaking from the aristocracy, he went instead to the temple we now call Eihei-Ji.

Though Dogen was philosophical and intellectual compared to Shinran or Nichiren, even he preached that the people should do zazen rather than read books. As *Shobo Genzo* shows us, the disciplines Dogen established were quite severe. He strictly regulated every move of daily life, and governed all aspects of life by the principle of action. Deeds and action were of the utmost importance.

It is in this respect that Kamakura Buddhism differed most from Heian Buddhism. During the Heian period Kukai and Saicho did preach action, of course, but not as it was done in Kamakura Buddhism. When we read the poems of *Shin Kokin Waka Shu*, compiled during the Kamakura period, even the way they express the inconstancy of life carries a sense of urgency.

This carried over into the treatment of the flower. In *Kokin Waka Shu* flowers fall with flowery abandon, inviting all to look up and sigh with admiration. But in *Shin Kokin Waka Shu* we are made to feel the flowers fall with intensity and fervor. In this way social conditions affect the manner in which things are perceived.

Zeami's *Fushi Kaden* also reflects this attitude. In it he writes mostly of his training methods, after first concisely stating the esthetic he had developed in his pursuit of the art of Noh. This book, in fact, was written for a particular person, not necessarily his own son, but someone Zeami considers deserving of the secret of his art.

This is the nature of the so-called *Densho* (*Secrets of Art*) in general. Zeami himself clearly says as much at the end of his: that the master will not pass on the secrets of his art to another, not even to his son, unless the recipient is qualified. In this book of strict discipline the word "flower," as I have said, appears over one hundred times and is used in many different ways.

Zeami considered *Shin Kokin Waka Shu* very important, and his works for the Noh stage were greatly influenced by the *Tale of the Heike* as well. Both books crystalize the inconstancy of life in succinct language. It is important to note that Zeami used lines from these books as part of his Noh plays, and that against the background of life's transience he used the term "flower" to explain his theatrical esthetics.

For him "flower" in *Fushi Kaden* mostly represented the qualities of "rarity" and "splendor." He placed considerable importance on these two qualities, but they must be seen in the same historical context as that in which the concept of "flower" developed.

Working within the theatrical art of Noh, where even the best drama might fail to please an audience unless its staging was also stimulating, Zeami was led to emphasize the importance of "rarity" and "splendor." He paid great attention to the reaction of the audience at a Noh performance. At that time the audience consisted mostly of aristocrats and warriors of the Ashikaga Clan, not necessarily the possessors of refined artistic tastes. Some would be easily distracted, chat with friends, even drink during a performance. The performers might be less than totally committed or highly skilled. This was certainly true in Kyogen, the comic interludes for the Noh theater, as documented in the early Edo-period book *Waranbe Gusa* by Okura Toraaki.

These are the conditions Zeami faced. How could he capture an audience's attention?

First of all, the Noh drama itself had to be of rare quality. Zeami explained this quality as "flowers blooming from a rock." A rock does not bloom, of course, but Zeami insists that Noh performers must possess a quality just that rare: part of his strategy for overwhelming an audience not necessarily inclined to art.

He also used the term *hana* to designate something exquisitely elegant, or youth, or even old age, and the evolution of these concepts around the word "flower" have helped form the Japanese esthetic sense.

FLOWERS IN *MAN'YO SHU*: *UME* BLOSSOMS AT THEIR FULLEST

Now I will discuss poems about flowers, based on the concepts we have just explored. This first poem is quite famous.

> *Aoni yoshi Nara no Miyako wa saku hana no*
> *niou ga gotoku ima sakari nari*

> The capital of Nara
> with red pillars and white walls
> glows with life
> like radiant flowers

Ono no Oyu
Man'yo Shu 328

The *ni* in *aoni* is vermilion clay, from which vermilion pigment was derived. The ancients used vermilion to color temple gates and ships, and to prevent rot. In those days decorative materials were used for reasons beyond simple decoration, and vermilion was useful as well as esthetically attractive. For this we must admire the esthetics of the ancients: their colors were often as practical as pleasing to the eye.

What is most functional is usually esthetically pleasing as well. I can think of hardly anything that is highly practical, yet very unpleasant to the senses. In this way practicality is closely related to beauty. Yet many people today see nothing wrong in using colors that appeal to them, whether or not those colors make any practical sense. We even find this attitude among some artists.

Personally, I believe that functionality carries its own beauty, but beauty alone cannot achieve functionality.

The capital city of Nara is full of functional beauty. Novel ideas and objects, such as Buddhist statues, for example, arrived in Japan from China and Korea during the Nara period. The people must have been awed by their grandeur.

Nara has had a statue of Buddha since around the time of Emperor Suiko. Statues of Buddha during the Hakuho (672-685) and Tenpyo (729-748) periods, the most prosperous times of the Nara era, were as tall as 4.85 meters (16 feet) standing, 2.5 meters (eight feet) seated. Since the earlier Buddhist statues came from China or Korea, they had continental features, making their facial expressions appear quite austere to the Japanese. The people who looked up at them must have thought them fearsome.

Buddhism implied the existence of a new life for the people of that time, and once the emperor converted to the religion it took root in Japanese soil.

The following poem was written in praise of Nara as seen in this light, with the capital at the peak of glory as its flowers glowed in the sun. These flowers must be cherry blossoms, seen amid the inexpressible beauty of a grove of trees in full flower. The whole capital would be in blossom, and since flowers represented the vitality of life, this is really a poem in praise of Nara culture.

> *Otomera ga kazashi no tame ni*
> *miyabio ga kazura no tame to*
> *shiki maseru kuni no hatate ni*
> *saki ni keru sakura no hana no nioi wa mo ana ni*
> > *[hanka]*
> *kozo no haru aerishi kimi ni koi ni teshi*
> *sakura no hana wa mukae kerashi mo*

Cherry blossoms --
maidens use them to ornament their hair
men of taste wear them as garlands
throughout the country of our emperor's august rule

the flowers bloom, their fragrance prevails
[envoy]
Since they first saw you last spring
the very flowers have yearned for you
once more they bloom to welcome you

Wakamiya no Ayumaro
Man'yo Shu 1429-30

Maidens break off twigs of cherry blossoms to decorate their hair. Men of taste and elegance, while they seem to while away their lives, take a detached view of themselves, the world around them, and the times they live in. They crown their heads with wreaths of blossoms. (Such artless, elegant practices were prevalent in the Nara period.) The poem goes on to praise Nara culture by saying how beautiful and fragrant are the cherry blossoms under the reign of the emperor.

The envoy to this poem is: The flowers first saw you last spring; since then they have been in love with you; those flowers are again blooming to receive you. The author uses cherry blossoms to praise life in bloom. Here in the Man'yo period is the early stage of historical progression in the people's attitude toward flowers, when flowers were viewed as something graceful and full of life in its proudest phase.

Sakazuki ni ume no hana ukabe omou dochi
nomite no nochi wa chirinu tomo yoshi

We float *ume* petals
in our sake cups
to share our thoughts
to share our drinks
to our heart's content
then we'll have no regrets
even when the flowers are gone

Otomo no Sakanoue no
Iratsume
Man'yo Shu 1656

During the *Man'yo Shu* period *ume* was popular, fashionable, and exotic. People held parties to drink sake and view the *ume* blossoms. The poet is talking to the flowers: drinking sake, we catch your petals in our cups as they drift down. We do want you to remain. Yet, after this party is over, we won't complain even if you are gone.

This poem does refer to *ume* petals falling, but in fact the poet implores the *ume* blossoms to keep blooming. The poem does not communicate a sense of transiency; its motive is luxuriant pleasure. Ume blossoms are as alive as men, and as the friends share the pleasure of drink they invite the blossoms to join in, again revealing the *Man'yo* attitude toward flowers.

CHERRY BLOSSOMS, FALLING IN GRACEFUL GRANDEUR,
TAKE CENTER STAGE IN *KOKIN WAKA SHU*

We have no details about the poet Ono no Komachi, but she had been dead for decades in the early part of the tenth century when *Kokin Waka Shu* was compiled.

> *Hana no iro wa utsuri ni keri na itazura ni*
> *waga mi yo ni furu nagame seshi mani*

> The color of the flowers
> has faded to nothing
> as I have passed my life
> in melancholy
> watching the long rains fall

> Ono no Komachi
> *Kokin Waka Shu* 113

Komachi, along with Narihira, was one of the Six Great Medieval Poets who were active during the period that followed Man'yo Shu and preceded *Kokin Waka Shu*.

Komachi and Narihira were towering figures in *Kokin Waka Shu*, and their poems bridge the two collections of poetry. Already, for these poets, flowers are for falling.

Sakurabana chiri kaikumore
oiraku no komu to iu naru michi magou gani

Cherry blossoms!
fall in torrents and cloud over
the path Old Age is said to follow
so he will not find his way

Ariwara no Narihira
Kokin Waka Shu 349

This poem was composed for the then prime minister Fujiwara Mototsune on the occasion of his fortieth birthday. Mototsune was an adopted son of Fujiwara Yoshifusa, a key figure of the second generation of the prosperous Fujiwara family. For a song celebrating such an important man this poem is quite out of the ordinary, because it tells the cherry blossoms to fall in a frenzy, to make a cloud.

Poems were recited aloud at that time, so the hearers must have been shocked at the first part of this verse. Talk of "clouding over" is totally inappropriate at a time of celebration. Since cherry blossoms do fall in a cascade, however, the poet is asking the blossoms to block the path Old Age is traveling -- a powerful conception following the poem's initial shock. I consider this to be among the best of Narihira's poems. The fact that Narihira was audacious enough to sing it at a celebration party proves he was no ordinary poet.

Haru no no ni wakana tsumamu to koshi mono o
chirikau hana ni michi wa madoinu

In the spring field
we came
to pick young greens

but the flowers fell so thick
we lost our way

Ki no Tsurayuki
Kokin Waka Shu 116

Ki no Tsurayuki, the leading figure of the prime of the *Kokin Waka Shu* period, was two or three generations younger than Narihira. Tsurayuki probably had Narihira's poem in mind when he composed this piece. Narihira was long dead, of course, but as compiler of *Kokin Waka Shu* Tsurayuki was familiar with his poetry, and he was a master at stealing others' best ideas. Stealing sounds ominous, but it takes talent to find what is superb in others and incorporate it into your own work, as poets need to do.

The ceremonial picking of green shoots was a New Year's custom during the Man'yo Period. Young girls wore beautiful robes and people enjoyed watching them in the fields. Even in *Shin Kokin Waka Shu*, when they no longer gathered shoots in this ceremonial manner, they sing about picking greens in the Kasuga fields. Clearly this is a poetic adaptation of the *Man'yo Shu* tradition.

The young greens shooting out of the early spring soil are full of life's force. People picked seven different greens, believing that eating them would keep disease away, or even prolong life. The custom originated in China and has carried through to our present day ritual of eating porridge with seven greens at New Year's.

Tsurayuki's poem is in this tradition -- he is not necessarily recounting his own experience. Those who came to gather fresh young greens in celebration of Spring have lost their way because of the cascading flower petals blocking their view. This does not bother them, of course; on the contrary, they enjoy it. The poem features both the picking of greens and the viewing of falling petals, two great esthetic pleasures of Spring. It is obviously in tune with the celebratory spirit of Narihira's poem.

Yadori shite haru no yamabe ni netaru yo wa
yume no uchi nimo hana zo chirikeru

As I sojourned overnight
in the mountain village in Spring—
cherry blossoms cascading
even in my dreams

Ki no Tsurayuki
Kokin Waka Shu 117

Tsurayuki spends a night on a mountainside in springtime. Even in his dreams the cherry blossoms fall profusely. Though these are flowers in the act of falling they are once again presented as a spectacular sight.

The following poem by Priest Sosei is in the same spirit.

Miwataseba yanagi sakura o kokimazete
miyako zo haru no nishiki narikeru

Spread out before our eyes
willows and cherry blossoms
all woven together
our capital is a tapestry of Spring

Priest Sosei
Kokin Waka Shu 56

This poem, set in Kyoto, makes a good contrast with our first poem, the one by Ono no Oyu. The poet, being a priest, is probably at Mt. Hiei, looking down over the capital city. He sees young willow leaves as well as cherry blossoms, their green and light pink blending together, turning the city into a woven tapestry. These are not just falling flowers -- they are the flowers of prosperous times.

Nokori naku chiru zo medetaki sakurabana
arite yo no naka hate no ukereba

Fortunate are the cherry blossoms
that fall all at once

leaving no trace
since the end is too depressing
if one lingers in this world

> Anonymous
> *Kokin Waka Shu* 71

Here the poet focuses on the falling of cherry blossoms. Better that they all fall at once, he says, since seeing them fall little by little would make him dejected. Yet he does not associate the falling with melancholy. Since flowers must fall, let it be spectacular.

Hisakata no hikari nodokeki haru no hi ni
shizugokoro naku hana no chiru ramu

The eternal sun shines in peace and calm
on a spring day
Why do the cherry blossoms flutter down
so restlessly

> Ki no Tomonori
> *Kokin Waka Shu* 84

On a spring day, with the sun shining calmly on the garden, why do the cherry blossoms fall in such agitation? The poet concentrates on the falling of petals on a calm spring day. His concern stems from his love of the flowers.

Hana no iro wa kasumi ni komete misezu tomo
ka o dani nusume haru no yama kaze

Spring breezes from the hill!
even if you let the mist hide
the color

of the cherry blossoms
at least steal us their scent
Yoshimine no Munesada (Priest Henjo)
Kokin Waka Shu 91

On the surface the poet is asking the spring breeze to at least steal away and bring forth the scent of the cherry blossoms when it has carried in mist to block the flowers from view. But in *Kokin Waka Shu* nature was often used to represent human affairs, and this poem is generally interpreted as a love poem. The poet implores a young woman to at least let him hear from her in response to his love letter, even if she is hidden away from him by the mist. The mist in this case may be her mother, stubbornly guarding the daughter, while the scent is her letter. The spring breeze is her maid, the go-between who carries the letter.

Priest Henjo must have been a lady's man before he became a priest; he left many witty poems soliciting love, and was the embodiment of the love of amorous ventures idealized during the high point of the Heian Period.

As these poems show, throughout the Heian Period flowers, even though they must fall, are always spectacular. Now let us look at *Shin Kokin Waka Shu.* The poems in this anthology are not all from the Kamakura Period; a number are from earlier times. And although this makes it difficult to generalize, we can discern a difference between the two eras.

TRANSIENCE, MUTABILITY, AND FLOWERS

Yamazato no haru no yugure kite mireba
iriai no kane ni hana zo chirikeru

As I visit the mountain village
on an evening in spring
the cherry blossoms fall
to the tolling bell
at the close of day

Priest Noin
Shin Kokin Waka Shu 116

Priest Noin's work dates from just after the compilation of *Kokin Waka Shu*, well before the time of *Shin Kokin Waka Shu*. Seeking a special atmosphere, the poet travels to a peaceful mountain village. It is an evening in Spring and the mood is relaxed and genial. As he arrives at the village the temple bell tolls the close of day, and the flowers fall as if in response to the bell. By this time it was common practice to compose a poem on falling cherry blossoms, but Priest Noin was especially deft at creating a stage setting.

In addition to the flowers falling we have an evening in a mountain village, plus the end-of-day bells. In the evening mountain villages are often visited by haze, which increases the serenity of the scene. In a setting that combines time and sound we hear the bells tolling -- probably a few nearby temple bells mixing and echoing -- and we see flowers fall. Priest Noin was typical of the poets of his time in his effort to create dramatic settings for poetry.

This poem by Priest Noin is still easygoing. The next poem by Princess Shikishi, however, is typical of the Kamakura era. As noted earlier in this book, Princess Shikishi comes of a royal line. Daughter of ex-Emperor Goshirakawa and survivor of civil wars in which she lost many of her relatives, she served as a vestal virgin at the Kamo Shrine throughout her childhood and youth. Her concerns were far removed from flowery love, as one would expect; all of her poems reveal a mind steeped in deep sorrowful thoughts.

> *Hakanakute suginishi kata o kazoureba*
> *hana ni mono omou haru zo heni keru*

> As I count up the years
> that have flown away
> I have seen many springs
> while yearning under the cherry blossoms
>   Princess Shikishi
>   *Shin Kokin Waka Shu* 101

I am counting the years that have passed away. Every year I have been deep in thought, pondering the cherry blossoms. I grow older as all these springs go by.

The flowers (cherry blossoms) here are tied to the passage of time in its coming and going. They are also inseparably related to how she has spent her womanhood. In this sense this poem is deeply introspective.

> *Kaze kayou nezame no sode no hana no ka ni*
> *kaoru makura no haru no yo no yume*

> The wind passes
> as I awaken, rousing
> the scent of the flowers
> from my sleeves. My pillow takes on the scent
> of my spring night dreams
>
> Shunzei's Granddaughter
> *Shin Kokin Waka Shu* 112

On a spring dawn she wakes up to the passage of the breeze. The fragrance of cherry blossoms drifts through the sleeves of her robe, scenting her pillow and reminding her of her dreams of the night before. But now it's morning, and the dreams have vanished like the beautiful scent of the flowers.

Here we have the wind, the scent, and her dreams all vanishing into thin air. At first glance it all seems flowery and beautiful, but this poem does not portray real life; rather the poet is intent on creating a beautiful phantom with words. However solid this creation may be, the phantom too must fade. The words work their magic to present an unearthly dream in which only the poetic form has any substance. The scent of flowers is treated in the most decadent fashion at this stage in Japanese poetry.

> *Aware nari wagami no hate ya asamidori*
> *tsui niwa nobe no kasumi to omoeba*

> Pity!
> to think of my end
> to become the mist that floats

over the early green
of the burning grounds

Ono no Komachi
Shin Kokin Waka Shu 758

The poem does not deal with flowers but it does deal with things that fade away. In this respect it is like the poem by Shunzei's granddaughter.

This is usually read as a reference to the time of cremation. After death, says the poet, my body will be burned, and smoke will rise like mist over the fields. I will fade away as mist over the early green of spring fields. That is the end of my life. What a pity.

That's the most common interpretation. But somehow it sounds too pat. It's true that the poem expresses a sense of transience, but we can also read it as having more immediate application: she feels that if she simply walked into the misty field she might soon fade away with the mist. Between the Heian and the Kamakura Eras women's poetry became obsessed with the sense of transiency. Ono no Komachi lived in the early part of the Heian Period, but she had an unusual sense of the impermanence of the world. Because of that, perhaps, many of her poems were included in *Shin Kokin Waka Shu*.

Yononaka o omoeba nabete chiru hana no
wagami o satemo izuchi kamo semu

As I ponder on the world
all is flowers that must fall
If such is my fate
what, then, should I do with myself?

Priest Saigyo
Shin Kokin Waka Shu 1470

As he views the world, all people and all things fall away like flowers. His own physical self is doomed to the same fate. What, then, should be his purpose? Thus Saigyo ponders his lot in the world and his future in terms of the flowers of the world. Being a priest, Saigyo is of course influenced by the Buddhist view of the world as transient.

Kaze ni nabiku Fuji no kemuri no sora ni kiete
yukue mo shiranu waga omoi kana

Smoke from Mt. Fuji
drifts in the wind, fades into the sky
neither does my yearning
know where it leads me

Priest Saigyo
Shin Kokin Waka Shu 1613

"*Omoi*," the Japanese word for yearning, can also mean thought, and it carries the sound of the word fire (*omo-hi*, where *hi* means fire). This could be the volcanic fire of Mt. Fuji or a fire kindled and cherished in his heart. Neither thought nor yearning nor fire has any destination. Just as the smoke drifts off into thin air, the poet could be wondering about his own destiny. Or, as some see it, he could be yearning for the state of *satori*, the Buddhist's ultimate awareness.

Nani to kaya kabe ni ounaru kusa no nayo
sore nimo taguu waga mi narikeri

What would you call it --
the weed that grows on the wall?
I liken my life to it

Koka Mon'in
Shin Kokin Waka Shu 1788

A woman as noble as Koka Mon'in is comparing herself to a a weed growing on a stone wall.

Nagaraeba mata konogoroya shinobaremu
ushi to mishi yo zo ima wa koishiki

Once I've lived longer
I may cherish this time of my life
since now I yearn for times
that in the past depressed me

Kiyosuke no Ason
Shin Kokin Waka Shu 1843

The poet views the present times as sorrowful and depressing, but if he lives longer he might reminisce happily about them. The poet has a bleak outlook on his future. Kiyosuke, an accomplished scholar, was nearly blind in his later years, which might have contributed to his pessimism.

Negawakuba hana no moto nite haru shinamu
sono kisaragi no mochizuki no koro

If my wish were granted I would
die under the cherry blossoms
in spring under the full moon
of the Second Month

Priest Saigyo
Shin Kokin Waka Shu 1845

This is also a very famous poem, first anthologized in *Shin Kokin Waka Shu* but later deleted from it by ex-Emperor Gotoba. Saigyo actually died on the full moon of February by the lunar calender (early April by our calendar).

Yononaka wo omoi tsuranete nagamureba
munashiki sora ni kiyuru shirakumo

As I ponder deep and long
on the things of this world
a white cloud fades
into the great void of the sky

> Fujiwara Shunzei
> *Shin Kokin Waka Shu* 1846

As the poet thinks of the affairs of the world, they are like a wispy cloud that fades into the air: not a poem on flowers, but typical of Shunzei. Shunzei is more a Heian than a Kamakura poet -- in fact, he is the greatest of the later Heian poets. Later he became a priest, and composed Buddhist-inspired poems as superb as his secular work.

Kururu ma mo matsubeki yo kawa
adashino no sueha no tsuyu ni arashi tatsu nari

Are we spared even for a brief moment
while the sun sets?
A storm rises over the dew on the tips of leaves
in Adashino, the burial grounds

> Princess Shikishi
> *Shin Kokin Waka Shu* 1847

Do we have any time, even a short time, before the sun sets? No. Life is like the dew blown by the wind over a burial ground. Adashino is an actual site of burial field in Sagano, on the outskirts of Kyoto. But the word also implies a commonplace, useless or worthless sort of field. Life is like the dew, blown away by the wind without ever seeing day's end.

Shizukanaru akatsuki gotoni miwataseba
mada fukaki yo no yumezo kanashiki

Every dawn in utter quiet
I look around to see
that the world is still in deep night
and my dream, this world, is painful

Princess Shikishi
Shin Kokin Waka Shu 1970

This poem's theme is taken from Buddhist scripture. Every dawn, when all is total silence, the poet wakes up and looks around in a serene state of mind. The world is still completely dark. In such darkness she hardly knows if she is alive. She wonders if this too could be a dream, and this thought pains her.

Yami harete kokoro no sora ni sumu tsuki wa
nishi no yamabe ya chikaku naruramu

When the darkness lifts
the moon lingers brightly in my mind's sky
It must now be near the mountain ridges
of the Western Land

Priest Saigyo
Shin Kokin Waka Shu 1979

This poem is placed at the end of the collection, which means that the compilers thought it embodied the spirit of *Shin Kokin Waka Shu*. The compilers were ex-Emperor Gotoba, Teika, and other poets. Ex-Emperor Gotoba initiated a reckless attempt at political coup; when it failed he was exiled to Oki Island, where he spent the rest of his life. Even in exile on the island he never stopped revising his selections for *Shin-Kokin Waka Shu*. In selecting this poem by Priest Saigyo the ex-Emperor must have tried to pour his own essence into the volume. He himself would die in exile.

The poem is highly philosophical: "*sumu tsuki*" means both the bright moon and the moon as it exists in the mind. As the mind's dark sky clears, the bright moon that sojourns there comes closer to the mountains of the West, the Pure Land where Buddha lived.

So we see that flowers and the moon, two of the key symbols in Japanese thought, carry a spiritual significance in *Shin Kokin Waka Shu* that is drastically different from how they were treated in *Kokin Waka Shu*, the poetry anthology of the previous era.

As we moderns talk about flowers and the moon, each of us must ask ourselves in what ways we are using these terms. Words such as flower or moon have become entities each of which encompasses a Japanese thought. As one tries to use the word "flower," for example, on an important occasion, one must realize the roots that word has in tradition, and how that particular use renews it.

Chapter Six

IN PRAISE OF NOW: HEIAN POETRY

Poetry is written with words. In Japan those words did not change much for a very long time, yet the poetry displayed fundamental differences from era to era.

An era makes a difference. The simple word era can refer to everything created by a particular race within a certain historical context, the sum of the events that society experienced, all the peculiarities of an age.

In Japanese poetry we have not only *waka* but also *haikai*, *tanka* (an updated mode of *waka* that began in the Meiji Era), and the modern *haiku* (*haikai* in more up-to-date dress). We also have free verse, or modern poetry, which by contrast with the others has only a century of history behind it.

If we examine these poetic modes we see that each changes every five or ten years. If we could look ahead we might see in the next century or so a total negation of certain poetic views that have prevailed for the past one or two hundred years.

It is on this basis that I will use *waka* and *haikai* for case studies in a consideration of changing poetic points of view. Even with the discussion limited to these two forms we will see how the era in which poets live changes their poetic outlook.

> *Yadori shite haru no yamabe ni netaru yo wa*
> *yume no uchi nimo hana zo chiri keru*
>
> As I sojourned overnight
> in the mountain village in Spring —

cherry blossoms cascading

even in my dreams

Ki no Tsurayuki

In the last chapter I discussed this poem in terms of "flowers;" here I will expand on this reading.

The poet does not tell us why he visited this mountain village. He might have gone to the temple to offer prayers, or maybe he went on an excursion to collect spring greens, as aristocrats often did. On that evening the cherry blossoms fell even in his dreams, he says.

The poet celebrates the spectacular fall of the cherry blossoms by emphasizing their presence in his dreams. The poem refers not to one cherry tree, but to the beauty of a whole mountainside of cherry trees letting their pale pink-white petals fall in the wind.

For about a week each spring whole mountainsides are covered with cherry blossom petals cascading like a snowfall. The falling blossoms practically flood the air -- and the poet's dreams.

The aristocracy had consolidated its position by the close of the first part of the Heian Era, the period when Tsurayuki lived. In this settled society Tsurayuki never managed to achieve high social standing. While the gap between his social rank and his literary worth may have kept him from complete fulfillment, he still must have been satisfied with the fine reputation he held as a man of letters.

As a man of letters and an aristocrat of the Heian Era, engulfed in a spectacular sea of falling cherry blossoms, he did not resist the magnificence of the scene, but opened to the joy of participating in his times. Face to face with any aspect of Nature the Heians would adopt an attitude quite different from the realistic stance of a modern poet. When the Heians try to express their observations they do so in a way that folds their position as part of the aristocracy into the texture of their perceptions. They see the natural and the human as always overlapping. Most of the Heian poets sang this way.

When Ki no Tsurayuki speaks of the beautiful blossoms dominating even his dreams we can read his statement as indicating satisfaction with the boundaries of his society and his world. This is the attitude *Kokin Waka Shu* valued, and in this sense all the poetry in this anthology is essentially celebratory. People die, of course, and a section called "Dirge" is included in the anthology, but most poems in the anthology are concerned with celebration, the major premise of the era.

The anthology avoids the dark side of human life, including most pain or misery, in part because it was *chokusen*, "compiled by the emperor." In reality the emperor himself rarely made the actual selection; he usually assigned a chosen few to compile it. But this is still a limiting factor in the history of Japanese poetry. Many fine poems were not included in these court anthologies, and we must look for them in the private collections of individual poets. The basic purpose of court anthologies was to praise the reign of an emperor for its prosperity and stability, to wish the emperor longevity, to celebrate his era. This purpose inspired every anthology's creation.

Though court anthologies are not truly representative of all the Japanese poetry of their era, they are nevertheless important as the embodiment of what everyone believed poetry should be. In this sense they established the main poetic tradition of the nation. *Kokin Waka Shu* was a model of their type, and by extension Tsurayuki's poem can be considered the prototype of a Spring poem.

Shin Kokin Waka Shu was compiled 300 years after *Kokin Waka Shu*. By then the Heian aristocrats' jubilant celebration of their own existence had long vanished, and a few powerful warrior families had risen from regional clans to take over political authority. The aristocrats, who had boasted during the Heian era of their exclusive claim to culture, had lost their standing, and a sense of the urgency of their situation was growing stronger among them by the day. These were the times when Princess Shikishi lived.

We have already glanced at her life and work. Daughter of ex-Emperor Goshirakawa, tragic witness to the death of many of her kin in civil war, she spent much of her life as a vestal virgin at the Kamo Shrine. Like the Ise Shrine, the Kamo Shrine was held in high esteem by the court. Imperial Princesses were sent there to become vestal virgins, often before they were 10 years old, and remained in that role throughout the Emperor's reign. One vestal virgin in each Emperor's reign seemed to be the rule: she would serve the deity on behalf of the Emperor, becoming, in a sense, bride to the deity. Vestal virgins were sacred and inviolable, but led a very lonely life.

Man'yo Shu records a poem written by Okuni no Himemiko, a vestal virgin at the Ise Shrine, on the occasion of a visit by her younger brother, Prince Otsu no Miko. She had already been at Ise for a long time when her brother, soon to be arrested and executed during a power struggle at court, traveled across mountains to pay his visit. If we didn't know the circumstances, we could mistake her parting poem to him as a song to her lover -- which brings home how isolated these vestals were from contact with men.

Princess Shikishi spent more than ten years of her youth in this same situation. Kamo Shrine was close to the Capital but the restrictions placed upon her there totally defined her young life. This condition contributed to a legend of a secret love affair between her and Fujiwara Teika, 10 years her junior and the greatest poet of his time. The legend caught the popular fancy, becoming the basis of the Noh play *Teika Kazura*.

INCREASED INTROSPECTION, MORE SONGS OF LONELINESS

Princess Shikishi's situation has attracted much attention over the ages. Of the five poems I will consider here, the first is in *Shin Kokin Waka Shu* and the last in *Shoku Gosen Shu*. The other three are not anthologized in the imperial collections.

> *Ato mo naki niwa no asaji ni musubohore*
> *tsuyu no soko naru matsumushi no koe*

> My yard is rank with weeds
> where no footsteps are heard
> Trapped in the weeds
> under the dew
> a cricket cries

On the surface a cricket is the center of this poem. We also see a yard rank with weeds, indicating an absence of visitors. Under the weeds are dewdrops and the cricket crying in loneliness.

That is all. But underneath the surface there is another layer of emotion. As I said earlier, court poetry parallels human affairs with those of nature. In this case a woman is alone, without a man. Either he no longer loves her, or he has become indifferent to her, because she has grown older in the course of struggling through her relationship with him. Either way, here is a woman who is extremely lonely because no man visits to court her. She is trapped in the weeds where she knows no one will ever set foot.

The dew trapped in the weeds signifies tears, a common parallel in court poetry. Drenched with tears, she waits for her man, wasting away like a cricket in late autumn.

This, then, is a woman's sad love song. Contrast its point of view with that of the flower poem by Tsurayuki that I quoted earlier. Instead of offering the sweeping perspective of the side of a mountain, this poem pinpoints a cricket, the poet herself, in the dew, under the weeds. The viewpoint is narrowed to a sharp focus, conveying a serious psychological state.

This kind of sharp focus is not to be found in *Kokin Waka Shu*, but is frequent in *Shin Kokin Waka Shu*. Princess Shikishi's poems are the most striking examples:

> *Nokori naku ariake no tsuki no moru kage ni*
> *honobono otsuru hagakure no hana*

> Bathed in the light of
> the moon at dawn
> petals faintly fall
> hidden among leaves

The flowers behind the leaves are cherry blossoms. The moon bathes the whole yard in light. So far the author's viewpoint seems to replicate Tsurayuki's in its survey of the entire scene. The difference is that her attention is fixed on "faintly falling petals" that are "hidden" by the leaves. With blossoms falling all around, she focuses on one particular spot.

This is a skilled presentation, far more refined in terms of poetic technique than anything in *Kokin Waka Shu*. She tries to capture the beauty of flowers, but the leaves hide them. She seeks a beauty that is not apparent -- quite a departure from Tsurayuki's celebration of the spectacle of beauty in the falling flowers.

> *Yugiri mo kokoro no soko ni musubitsutsu*
> *wagami hitotsu no aki zo fukeyuku*

> Evening mist also curls
> at the bottom of my heart
> I am alone
> as the autumn deepens

The sharpened focus is apparent from the start: "Evening mist also curls / at the bottom of my heart." While mist normally spreads over a person's external world, in this poem it curls inside, at the bottom of her heart. Instead of spreading out it contracts in her heart as a knot of depression.

"I am alone / as the autumn deepens" had been a favorite poetic phrase since the days of *Kokin Waka Shu.* There is, for example, Oe no Chisato's well-known *waka*: "As I view the moon / countless memories come to mind / to draw me into sorrow / even though this autumn, this sense of desolation / is not mine alone."

Sometimes it seems the Japanese associate the autumn moon with sorrow just because of this verse. The noun *aki*, autumn, is also a play on the verb *aki*, which suggests that one is wearied with love affairs. In Oe no Chisato's poem his sense of aloneness is contrasted with innumerable thoughts that come to mind as he observes that he shares this autumn with many others in the world.

But in Princess Shikishi's case her attention is focused on her own solitude. Though she uses the same phrase, she speaks of an autumn that is hers alone, unknown to others. The poem resonates with the anxiety and sense of urgency that dominated the end of the Kamakura era, so completely opposed to the optimistic and celebratory tone that characterized the Heian.

> *Mishi koto mo minu yukusue mo karisome no*
> *makura ni ukabu maboroshi no uchi*

> What I have seen
> what I have yet to see
> are ephemera that float

above my pillow
in fleeting sleep

This is also a very sad poem. All the experiences she has had, plus the future she has not yet seen, are mere phantoms over her pillow during a brief existence. The poem is filled with weariness of life, as well as a deep sense of life's transiency.

Hito shirezu mono omou sode ni kurabebaya
michikuru shio no nami no shitakusa

Unknown to him, I pine for him,
and cry into my sleeves
drenched like weeds
under the waves
as the tide comes in

The woman is in love and in pain, and the man she loves is not even aware of it. As she wipes away her tears her sleeves get so wet that she compares them to shore weeds under the waves as the tide comes in. "Weeds under the waves" here has the same effect as "in fleeting sleep" in the last poem. The focus is narrow, inward, the antithesis of outward expansion. It is this characteristic that appeals to readers.

Princess Shikishi did not necessarily compose these poems in the throes of love and pain. The people of her time did not believe poetry should be composed out of personal experience; instead they worked within certain conventions.

Love poetry, for example, had its proper form, and every poet in or out of love was expected to follow it. At the other extreme a person in agony would not hesitate to write a celebratory song when the occasion required, following precedents in *Kokin Waka Shu* and shaping his expression to conform to models he found there. Though this may seem uncreative, it was the custom of the Heian period, when originality was a matter of little concern. One was part of a total society, and one would participate in the joy or sorrow of that society through poetry. The individual creative urge had little value in poetry written to be read at official functions.

MAN'YO SHU: MODEL OF SELF-EXPRESION DURING NAN-BOKU CHO

Princess Shikishi lived during the early years of the Kamakura Period. The Nan-boku cho period, when there were two competing emperors and courts, came next. This was followed by the Civil War and Muromachi periods.

During Nan-boku cho the aristocrats maintained high social standing and respectability but had no real power. In this peculiar period even the emperor's position was not secure, with two emperors reigning simultaneously. The dual reign came about when a pact between two royal brothers, that they and their sons would take turns in succeeding to the throne, was broken, and the sons each established a separate reign.

Waka by people who lived during the beginning of this period were collected in two Imperial Anthologies, *Gyokuyo Waka Shu* and *Fuga Waka Shu.*

Gyokuyo Waka Shu was compiled by Kyogoku Tamekane, a descendant of Fujiwara Teika and a representative poet of his time. He studied not only *Kokin Waka Shu* and *Shin Kokin Waka Shu*, as was usual then, but also, with considerable enthusiasm, *Man'yo Shu*. He was looking for a freer form of expression than he found in rule-ridden post-Heian Era *waka.*

His outlook brought him into sharp opposition with the Nijo family, also descendants of Fujiwara Teika. The Nijos stood for the preservation of the post-*Kokin Waka Shu* tradition, and they were intent on abiding by its rules. Tamekane, however, believed that *waka* would not survive without an infusion of fresh blood. So he studied the *Man'yo Shu.*

What did he find? First, a new landscape. The natural features of the Yamato Plain, so different from Kyoto Basin, are vividly captured in the *Man'yo Shu*. Second, he found a different poetic. Free from the rigid rules later imposed on poetry, people of the *Man'yo Shu* era could write to their own individual tastes. And finally he found a broader social spectrum. As the poems by frontier guards or farmers demonstrate, authorship was not limited to aristocrats. These conditions were novel in the eyes of Tamekane and his contemporaries, and he learned from them.

Tamekane served under Emperor Fushimi and his successors, and was a powerful political voice throughout. He was involved in political strife, was exiled twice, and died during his second exile. He was reported to be a daring, bold man. *Tsurezuregusa* recounts the reaction of a young aristocrat of the Fujiwara Clan on seeing Tamekane, hands bound behind his back, led down the major street of Kyoto like a common criminal. Watching this proud prisoner, the aristocrat decided this was how a real man should act. Tamekane refused to bow to the military, and had total confidence in his power as an aristocrat and man of letters.

SHIFTING THE FOCUS TO CHANGES IN NATURE

Tamekane's poetry, like the man, is very interesting. But here we are dealing with his influence in shaping the poetry of his age, and we can see it in the poetry of ex-Emperor Fushimi and ex-Empress Eifuku, as collected in *Gyokuyo Waka Shu* and *Fuga Waka Shu*.

Though *Fuga Waka Shu* was compiled after Tamekane's death, it is so close in tone to *Gyokuyo Waka Shu* that the two are often discussed together. Ex-Emperor Fushimi's work will help illustrate their poetics.

> *Yama no ha mo kiete ikue no yugasumi*
> *kasumeru hate wa ame ni narinuru*

> Layers of evening mist
> blur the outline of mountain ridges
> At its edge the mist turns into rain

The rising mist seems to erase the outline of the mountain ridge. The mountain itself becomes a blur, at the edge of which it is raining. That is all. By utilizing homonyms (*ikue*, layers; *ikue*, going) he captures the change from mist to rain. Nature here is not captured as a static presence, but presented as a process of swirling change.

In both collections the poets focus on change, and the poetry is full of movement and mutation.

> *Yoi no ma no murakumo zutai kage miete*
> *yama no ha meguru aki no inazuma*

> Through swiftly gathering evening clouds
> light flashes --
> autumn lightning
> skirts the mountain edges

The evening clouds, drifting through the sky, gather in layers. *Kage* can mean shadow or light. In this case it is the light of thunderbolts, coursing through the scattered clouds to reveal their outlines. The lightning moves along the mountain ridges. This is nature at its most dynamic, the unsettled air showered by lightning from all directions.

> *Tsuki ya izuru hoshi no hikari no kawaru kana*
> *suzushiki kaze no yuyami no sora*

> Is the moon coming out?
> the sheen of the stars is changing
> the wind is cool
> in the sky where dusk gathers

Is the moon coming out? The color of the stars seems to shift with the evening breeze. The stars must have looked like they were dimming in the face of the moon. The poet captures the delicate change in the evening darkness before moonrise.

These three poems show poets once more turning outward toward nature. During the Kamakura Period, an age filled with urgency and anxiety, the focus was on the internal universe. This was true not only of Princess Shikishi but also of many others; as one can see in the poems on flowers, their concern was always the inner self, even when the subject matter was nature. Priest Saigyo looked at the wispy smoke over Mount Fuji and said "I know not where my thoughts drift." He used nature to talk about his mind.

Ex-Emperor Fushimi's approach is quite different. His thoughts, indeed his own self, virtually disappear in his poetry. In a way the poets of his time function as eyes, with no interposing mind.

What should we make of this? Ex-Emperor Fushimi, who lived when the Imperial Family was under the protection of the Hojo family, did not exercise any real power. When the Mongol emperor of the Yuan Dynasty attempted to invade Japan, for example, the Japanese emperor did nothing. The only exception was ex-Emperor Kameyama: he went to the Ise Shrine to pray for the safety of the nation. The others showed no inclination to do even that much.

Towazugatari, meaning "Tales told without being asked," the autobiographical diary of a lady in waiting at the court, explains the way of life behind this attitude. Attributed to ex-Emperor Gofukakusa's concubine Nijo, it offers a stark picture of court life gone decadent, particularly in the relations between men and women.

Ex-Emperor Gofukakusa, whom Nijo served, was not in the least fazed when the huge Yuan Dynasty force massed to attack. He continued indulging in his daily pursuits of games and music, as if to say that this had nothing to do with him.

In effect ex-Emperor Gofukakusa raised Nijo from girlhood, then made her one of his favorite mistresses. Later she was shuttled from man to man. When she reached middle age she gave up this life, made a pilgrimage throughout Japan, and wrote a wholesome journal of her travels.

Nijo's diary of Kyoto court life paints it as completely empty. All the aristocrats had left were their names and ranks. The Shogunate, the actual center of political power, did not tamper with the court, so the courtiers were assured of a certain level of wealth, but they had nothing to do. Man-woman relationships became their central concern, and their craving for excitement made these relationships convoluted in the extreme. Ex-Emperor Gofukakusa, for example, gave Nijo, whom he loved, to other courtiers. The only one of them who truly loved her passionately was the ex-Emperor's younger brother, later a high priest. What strange times -- a priest falls in love with his brother's concubine and becomes obsessed with desire.

Perhaps the reason these poets had no interest in looking into their own minds was that they gave themselves up to the flow of their environment for the sake of securing momentary pleasure. In a sense, nature consoled them. Unlike Princess Shikishi, who condensed the outside world into a point inside her mind, they emptied their minds, put themselves at the mercy of nature, and made careful observations of changes in nature. Their descriptions of natural change are often pleasant, and the poetry in *Gyokuyo Waka Shu* and *Fuga Waka Shu* is surprisingly refreshing.

The Aristocratic Era was coming to an end, and this short-lived style was like a dying candle, shining with a last brilliance before snuffing out completely.

POETRY FOCUSING ON FRAGMENTATION

Ex-Empress Eifuku, sometimes thought to be Nijo's daughter, was the wife of Emperor Fushimi. We will consider four of her poems.

> *Yamamoto no tori no koe yori akesomete*
> *hana mo muramura iro zo mieyuku*

> Morning arrives with birdcalls
> At the foot of the mountain
> cluster by cluster
> the flowers show color

At the foot of the mountain birds begin to sing. In the first light of dawn cherry blossoms, which the darkness had hidden, start to show as patches of color. We have a stand of cherry trees, and the arrival of daylight illuminates some of its blossoms but not others. Our attention is directed to detailed patterns.

The poem deals with changes. Birds announce the dawn, then blossoms begin to show, some brightly lit, some still in the dark. The dynamics of nature are set forth clearly.

> *Hototogisu sora ni koe shite unohana no*
> *kakine mo shiroku tsuki zo idenuru*

> A cuckoo's call is in the sky
> over the fence where hydrangea blooms
> white
> The moon rises

I grew up with a children's song written around this poem (our primary school years were steeped in the traditions of what we called *Gyokuyo* and *Fuga*, among others). A cuckoo flies across the sky, calling once. On the ground the hydrangea blooms white over the fence. Beyond that fence, in the middle of the sky, the moon is rising. The sense of the arrival of summer, a seasonal change, is expressed by putting together a few of Nature's fragments.

Hana no ue ni shibashi utsurou yuzukuhi
iru tomo nashini kage kienikeri

The evening sun lingers a while
over the flowers
Before I know that the sun has set
the glow fades away

Suddenly, before she knows it, the sun goes behind the edge of the mountain, and with it the sunlight that seemed to linger over the flowers. Sunlight is normally portrayed as streaming down; one does not usually think of it disappearing. As is characteristic of this period, the poem captures sunlight as something transient. Once again natural objects are presented in the process of change.

Mahagi chiru niwa no akikaze mi ni shimite
yuhi no kage zo kabe ni kieyuku

In the yard where the bush clover sheds its petals
the autumn wind of weariness
chills me through
The sinking sun's glow
seeps into the wall

This is the song of the autumn wind. The wind blows through a yard where clover bushes shed their flowers and she feels autumn, the season of parting, draw ever closer. Then the evening sunlight seeps into the wall.

The concept of light "seeping into the wall" is remarkable. We often see the evening light move along a wall, but this noblewoman sees it quite differently. Surrounded by empty grandeur, unfulfilled, she stands absently somewhere in the Court, eyes fixed on the wall as the early autumn wind blows away the bush clover flowers. To her eyes the evening sun seems to be seeping into the wall. This is the exact reverse of Princess Shikishi's image, which also used the idea of seeping, but said things were seeping into her mind.

The image of seeping figures importantly in Japanese poetry from *Kokin Waka Shu* on. Fujiwara Teika, for example, often says "The wind of autumn ... / carries the color that seeps into me." This tradition continues right down to Basho, one of whose famed haiku reads: "Quiet / the cicada's cry / seeps into rocks."

As I noted earlier in this book the idea of seeping comes from the dyeing or coloring process. When indigo pigment is added to a pure white cloth, for example, the dye will penetrate the cloth and change its color. Hence the word is used to describe a situation where contact between two entities causes certain changes to occur. Japanese poets typically paid close attention to this process of change.

Ex-Empress Eifuku's concern for the light seeping into the wall, or for the light over the flowers fading away, stands squarely in line with this tradition. Emperor Fushimi and ex-Empress Eifuku wrote poetry typical of their time. It dwelled on change in physical location, on physical movement that implied the passage of time, and, by extension, the transiency of being. That sense of transiency runs through the poetry of *Gyokuyo Waka Shu* and *Fuga Waka Shu*.

Seen from this vantage point in the history of Japanese poetry, the poets of the preceding age of *Shin Kokin Waka Shu* centered their awareness on their own inner selves and, so to speak, fought for their lives within that limited battleground.

That intensity couldn't last. The interest of poets shifted once more, from introspection to attention to the outside world. But instead of returning to the global vision of *Kokin Waka Shu* they became preoccupied with the transiency and mutability of the outer world they were observing. This, too, is a sharper focus, influenced by the intense inner concentration of the previous poetic age.

To make the contrast clear, think of Ki no Tsurayuki's global celebration of a profusion of cascading blossoms in comparison to the way these later poets talked of blossoms falling in specific areas. The narrowing of the field of vision after Tsurayuki's time did lead to the introduction of a sense of movement in the next poetic period.

Consider, for example, the third poem of Emperor Fushimi quoted earlier. He starts with "Is the moon coming out? / the sheen of the stars is changing," and follows this with "the wind is cool / in the sky where dusk gathers." His eyes shift quickly from one object to the next.

In the first two lines attention is focused on the sheen of the stars. The *Shin Kokin Waka Shu* poets would have pursued this point further, but Emperor Fushimi shifts his attention to the wind. There is a slight disjuncture between the two halves of the poem. You could almost get the same effect by having two poets each write half of the poem, then put the results together.

Ex-Empress Eifuku similarly introduces several different objects into her Cuckoo poem, virtually guaranteeing a division of attention. Or take the case of the poem on the bush clover. The first part reads: "In the yard where the bush clover sheds its petals / the autumn wind of weariness / chills me through." Poets of the previous era might have stayed in this subjective world, ending the poem with an expression of their own feelings, but Eifuku sidesteps that approach. Rather than pursue her own inner feelings she brings in another natural object.

It almost seems as if these poets are trying their best not to reveal their feelings. From my point of view, this tendency heralds the next generation of poetry: the linked verse of the Muromachi era, and its successor, the *haikai* of the Edo Period, an extension of linked verse with its witty aspects emphasized.

Look at the two-part structure of these poems, with each part having a different tone. Instead of a personal, subjective viewpoint maintained straight to the end, the poets combine a few elements from the natural scene to console themselves. The next logical step is linked verse and *haikai*, that is, a collaborative process rather than individual creative effort.

Epilogue

CLASSIC FORM, MODERN REVIVAL

In this book I have often referred to *renga* (linked verse) and *haikai no renga* (linked *haikai*). Recent events have shown that these ancient forms retain their power to inspire poetry and unite poets, not just among the Japanese, but among people of many nationalities.

Before I recount the events that led me to this conclusion, let me summarize the formal structure and historical background of these two closely related forms of communal poetic expression.

Renga was very popular during the medieval Kamakura and Muromachi Eras. *Haikai no renga*, now called *renku*, was widely practiced during the Edo Period.

In both *renga* and *renku* the poetry is the product of collaboration among several authors. *Renga*, to take the earlier form first, originally developed as part of the *waka* tradition, with two people collaborating on a single *waka*. One poet undertook to write the first verse of five, then seven, then five syllables (5-7-5); the other did the second verse (7-7). When each had composed his part of the *waka*, they recited it in turn to make up one complete poem. This was called *tan-renga* (short linked verse), and we have examples of the practice from as far back as *Man'yo Shu*.

Today, however, when we talk about *renga* we usually refer to the more extended form in which the longer (5-7-5) and shorter (7-7) verses are alternately composed by two or more authors until they amount to one hundred linked verses (*hyakuin*). There were also other renga formats, such as *kasen* (36 verses), *yoyoshi* (44 verses), *gojuin* (50 verses), *senku* (10 volumes of 100 verses each), and *manku* (a series of ten *senku*).

Only very rarely does one poet compose the entire *renga*; it is usually the product of multiple participants. Each poet, in writing his assigned verse, responds to the preceding verse, striving to shift its viewpoint and feeling in his own direction. In doing so he must observe certain rules, called *shikimoku*, designed to preserve the harmony of the collaborative effort. These rules do not prevent him from searching for the wittiest, most individualistic possible connection with the preceding verse.

These basic characteristics also defined the later *haikai no renga*, which prevailed during the Edo Period.

The word *haikai* originally meant "humor, wit." While the *renga* of the Kamakura and Muromachi Era was a court literature closely tied to the *waka* tradition and its stress on classic elegance, the *haikai no renga* reflected the Edo Period's Renaissance atmosphere, filled with the vital energy and affirmation of life of a newly moneyed bourgeois. This poetry depicted the vitality and diversity of the new social order through wit and humor. The basic feature of *haikai no renga* is the pursuit of dynamic development, full of unexpected twists and amusing turns.

Interestingly enough, while *haikai no renga* thus gained complexity, it tended to adopt shorter formats. Where *hyakuin* (100 linked verses) was considered the orthodox length for classic *renga*, *kasen* (36 verses) was the most popular length for *haikai no renga*.

Basho and his disciples popularized the *kasen* format in the 17th century. The level of accomplishment they achieved set high standards very early on in the *haikai no renga* tradition. One century later the great painter and poet Buson and his disciples left us another body of fine work in the *kasen* format.

What makes this collaborative creation most interesting is the nature of its results. When two or more participants alternately compose the longer (5-7-5) or shorter (7-7) verses, they journey together through the 36 verses by many unexpected passageways. Working jointly, they venture into a realm of poetic creation of which a single poet, working alone, could never have dreamed.

It is well known that the initial 5-7-5 verse of this collaborative form came to be treated as an independent poem, the *haiku*, beloved even today by the Japanese. In the post-Meiji Era, the pre-modern period when individualism moved into the mainstream of Japanese literary thought, *haiku* began to be composed and read as an independent poem, while interest in *haikai no renga* gradually waned.

As I point out in the "Prologue" to this book, however, when we survey the entire history of poetry and literature in Japan it is clear that collaborative creation, evaluation, and appreciation of poetry is the lifeblood of Japanese poetry.

For this reason *haikai no renga*, or *renku*, has recently been attracting keen attention and a rapidly growing number of practitioners. I count myself among them. Since 1970 I have composed *renku* in collaboration with a number of novelists and poets. I have also experimented with a new linked verse form, using free verse in place of the earlier fixed lines of linked verse.

Perhaps most interestingly, I have collaborated in linked free verse with poets from a number of other countries, including the United States, France, West Germany, The Netherlands, and Finland.

To my great surprise and satisfaction I have found that participating in linked free verse composition allows me and my fellow poets from other countries to build close friendships almost immediately. I am sure that without this shared experience in linked free verse writing we would have remained mere acquaintances, and our relationships would have been superficial at best.

This experience has made me rethink the essence, the very spirit of linked verse as it underlies Japanese poetic history. It is important to recognize that from earliest times the classic Japanese verse structure of 5-7-5-7-7, along with its components 5-7-5 and 7-7, was respected, even venerated, as "a gift of words" which worked as a catalyst to forge ties among people. So the classic formal poetry we have been considering is actually a refined form of interpersonal communication. Its most highly developed manifestation is collaborative poetry writing and appreciation such as *uta-awase* (poetry competition), *renga*, and *renku*. These form a whole tradition of poetry that affects our view of poems composed in the classic tradition by individuals. As we have seen, court-commissioned anthologies of poetry by many hands such as *Kokin Waka Shu*, *Shin Kokin Waka Shu*, and *Gyokuyo Waka Shu* were long considered superior to "private" collections, the collected poems of a single poet.

To illustrate this point let us use the example of Basho. One of the best poets Japan ever produced, Basho never published a collection of his own poetry -- in fact, he probably never even considered the possibility. He concentrated on editing collections of collaborative work by himself and his school to exhibit the many facets of the new world of haikai they were building. Throughout his career he continued to guide his fine group of disciples and to publish anthologies of his school of *haikai*.

Basho's practice reveals his conviction that his own "solitary mind," rooted in his own isolation, was made most truly active and creative when supported by the lively response of others. In other words, the genuine creativity of a "solitary mind" materializes only in the middle of a "banquet."

Basho's insight retains its value to this day. Linked verse and linked free verse are not antiquated forms of poetry. On the contrary, they should be reevaluated as a means to go beyond the confines of today's poetry.

I agree with what Octavio Paz says in "The Moving Center," his introduction to *Renga* (Gallimard, 1971; English translation, *Renga*, George Braziller, NY), a book he wrote in 1969 in collaboration with Eduardo Sanguineti, Charles Tomlinson, and Jacques Roubaud. Paz discusses the potential contribution of *renga* to modern literature:

> Our attempt naturally enters into the tradition of modern western poetry. One could even say that it is a consequence of its dominant tendencies: the conception of writing as combined act, the narrowing of frontiers between translation and original work, the aspiration toward a collective (and not collectivist) poetry.

In practice, self-consciously isolated and independent modern poets are often shocked by the extent of mutual discovery generated when they work together to build their *renga*.

It works like this. Several poets from different countries, strangers to each other, sit at a table in a building for a full day or more and collaborate in creating poetry. Through this act of collaboration they quickly become familiar with each other, gain a deeper understanding of what each other's laughter or silence means, and witness aspects of the poetic process of each participant as they are revealed.

This experience would be very hard to come by in everyday life. Two aspects are of critical importance. First, each participant witnesses the others in the process of grappling with reality and giving it forms of expression in ways very different from his or her own. Second, each repeatedly and with increasing proficiency responds to the work of the others with his or her own work.

In *renga*, then, each poet matches his or her own individuality with that of other poets to achieve a heightened aesthetic understanding. This leads to a harmony and balance unattainable by any one individual.

I believe that the powerful magnetic field of Japanese classic poetry, where the "Solitary Mind" interacts with others at the "Banquet," will open new possibilities to contemporary poetry as well. It creates a provocative and stimulating environment for modern poetry: creating poems for attentive, sensitive readers who are alternately the creators of the poems in their own right.

APPENDIX

PRIMARY SOURCES FOR THIS BOOK

Described below are the classic works -- collections of poetry and books on esthetics -- most frequently cited in this text. They are listed in alphabetical order.

CHOSHU EISO
   A private collection of Fujiwara Shunzei's poetry.

FUGA WAKA SHU (1346)
   The 17th imperial anthology, edited personally by Ex-emperor Hanazono. A total of 20 volumes, containing over 2,200 pieces. Organized according to *Gyokuyo Waka Shu's* groupings, this collection is clearly influenced by that anthology.

GO SHUI WAKA SHU (1364)
   The fourth imperial anthology, compiled by Nijo Tametomo on command of ex-Emperor Go-Kogen. Contains 1,920 verses in 20 volumes.

GYOKUYO WAKA SHU (1312)
   The 14th imperial anthology, ordered by ex-Emperor Fushimi. Its 20 volumes contain approximately 2,800 poems. Organized according to each of the four seasons, plus celebratory, journey, love, miscellaneous and Buddhist-Shinto related categories. The style of the poems was fresh, breaking away from the preceding period of monotonous poetry. The editor, Kyogoku Tamekane, was the leading innovative poet of his day.

KADEN SHO (1420)

Also known as *Fushi Kaden*. A seven-volume work on Noh by the Noh Master Zeami. Zeami recorded and organized the theory of Noh set forth for him by his father, the Noh Master Kan'ami. This work expounds the concepts of *hana* (flower) and *yugen*. Famous as a general theory of art.

KOKIN WAKA SHU (905)

The first Imperial Anthology of Japanese style poetry (as opposed to Chinese style poetry, which had been considered the official standard for poetry up to that time). Compiled by Ki no Tsurayuki and three other poets under the Imperial order of Emperor Daigo.

This anthology established Japanese style poetry (*waka*) as a major genre in Japanese literature. Its 20 volumes contain 1,112 verses by 122 poets in 13 categories, including each of the four seasons, separation, travel, love, etc. The selection is generally characterized as elegant and refined. In both format and content, this anthology becomes a model for later collections of waka.

KORAI FUTEI SHO (1201)

Styles Ancient and Modern, a five-volume work by Fujiwara Shunzei, which he wrote for Princess Shikishi at her request. He discusses poetry from the *Man'yo Shu* to the *Senzai Waka Shu*.

MAIGETSU SHO (1219)

by Fujiwara Teika. Originally entitled *Letters of Master Teika*. A collection of Teika's discourses on the principles and practice of writing *waka*. Here Teika discusses 10 types of *waka*, and emphasizes the importance of *yugen* (depth, elegant allure) as the paramount esthetic achievement.

MAN'YO SHU (771-794)

The oldest collection of poetry in Japan. Its 20 volumes contain 4,500 verses, 90% of which are *tanka* (*waka*). The editors must have changed from one volume to the next, but Otomo no Yakamochi (718-785) seems to be primarily responsible for the selection. Collects works by all segments of the society from Emperors to beggars and prostitutes, spanning 300 years, and covering a geographic range from eastern and northern Japan to

Kyushu and Chugoku. *Man'yo Shu* is characterized by the open expression of the poets' genuine feelings.

SASAMEGOTO (1461)

by Priest Shinkei. Two volumes of dialogues on linked verse, covering its history, manners, styles, and methods.

SENZAI WAKA SHU (1187)

The seventh Imperial Anthology of *waka*. Compiled by Fujiwara Shunzei by the order of Ex-Emperor Goshirakawa. Its 20 volumes contain 1,285 verses by 387 poets. The selection is characteristically gentle and elegant in style, and many of the poems are enigmatic and moody.

SHIN KOKIN WAKA SHU (1205)

The 8th Imperial Anthology, compiled by Fujiwara Teika and others under orders from Ex-Emperor Gotoba. Its 20 volumes contain some 1,900 verses. It was an impressive attempt to re-create *Kokin Waka Shu*. Noted for its high technical refinement, which aimed at *yugen*, and at *en'rei*, elegance and enigmatic expression.

SHOBO GENZO (1231-1253)

95 vols written by Dogen, the founder of the Soto sect of Buddhism. It covers the teachings, philosophy, and scriptures of Buddhism, as well as the life of Zen priests in general.

INDEX OF POEMS
BY FIRST LINE

GENERAL INDEX

Adashino, 76, 77, 112
Antoku (Emperor), 75, 79
Ariwara no Narihira, 50, 102
Autumn, 43-46, 75, 81, 88, 119, 120, 124, 127-129
Awaré (pathos), 21, 67

Banquet, 12, 15, 16, 17, 28, 33, 34, 35,134, 135
Basho, 19, 28, 40, 47, 66, 94, 128, 132, 133
Baudelaire, 30
Blake (William), 28, 30
Blossoms, 39-41, 45, 46, 70, 72, 82, 93, 94, 98-102, 104-108, 111, 116, 119, 126-128
Breadth, 87, 90
Buddha, 46, 99, 112
Buddhism, 31, 47, 50, 67, 83, 89, 94-96, 99, 139
Buddhist, 37, 46, 67, 79, 80, 94-96, 99, 109, 112, 113
Buddhist-Shinto, 137

Chill, 45, 53, 81, 82
Chomei, Kamo no, 82
Christianity, 31, 50, 51
Cocteau, 28
Color, 15, 38, 39, 41-49, 67, 68, 70, 89, 98, 101, 105, 124, 126, 128
Colorless, 46, 70
Colorlessness, 44, 71
Colors, 14, 16, 37-42, 46, 47, 70, 71, 88, 95, 98
Cuckoo, 73, 127, 129

Dante, 50
Depth, 13, 67, 74, 79, 89, 90
Dew, 43, 45, 46, 60, 75, 77, 111, 118, 119
Dogen, 71, 96, 139
Dojin-zasshi (coterie magazine), 32
Dye, 40, 49, 128

Egocentrism, 52
Eifuku Mon-in, 43
Elegance, 40, 48, 71, 72, 100, 132, 139

Eluard, 28
Emaki (picture scrolls), 34
Esthetics, 66, 93, 94, 97, 98, 137
E-awase (picture competitions), 34

Fleeting, 28, 76, 84, 121
Flower, 32, 35, 41, 77, 93-99, 103, 114, 119, 138
Flowers, 38-40, 42, 44, 69, 70, 77, 88, 93-109, 112-114, 116, 119, 124, 126-128
Fuga Waka Shu, 122, 123, 126, 128, 137
Fushi Kaden (book on Noh esthetics; also see Kaden-sho), 97
Fushimi, 122, 123, 125, 126, 128, 129, 137

Gendai-shi (modern poetry), 27
Gofukakusa (Emperor), 125
Gosen Waka Shu, 118
Goshirakawa (Emperor), 75, 79, 107, 117, 139
Go Shui Waka Shu, 53, 87, 89, 137
Gotoba (ex-Emperor), 79, 80, 111, 113, 139
Gyokuyo Waka Shu, 122, 123, 126-128, 133, 137

Haikai, 28, 33, 66, 93, 115, 129, 131, 132, 133
Haikai-no-renga, 93, 131-133
Haiku, 11, 27-32, 34, 35, 94, 115, 128, 132
Hana, 43, 44, 72, 76, 81, 93, 94, 98-103, 105-108, 111, 115, 119, 126, 127, 138,
Hanazono (ex-Emperor), 44, 137
Haru (Spring), 72, 99, 102-108, 111, 115
Heian, 40, 51, 58, 59, 63, 71, 75, 79, 80, 85-89, 93-96, 106, 106, 112, 115-117, 120-122
Henjo, Priest, 106
Hokkekyo (Saddharmapundarika sutra), 46, 95
Honkatori, 89
Hukakusa (Emperor), 81
Hyakunin Isshu, 34

Impermanence, 109
Inconstancy, 74, 94, 96
Iratsume, Kasa no, 57, 59, 60, 61, 100
Iro, 16, 37-39, 45, 46, 49, 101, 105, 126
Ise, 61, 117, 125

OOKA MAKOTO

Ooka Makoto was born February 16, 1931, in Shizuoka, Japan. His father was an educator and *tanka* poet.

On graduating from the Tokyo University Department of Literature in 1953 he joined the Yomiuri Newspapers as a reporter. He taught Japanese literature at Meiji University 1965-87. Since 1988 he has been Professor of Japanese Literature at the National University of Fine Arts and Music.

Ooka is the author of 18 books of poetry. His 15-volume collected works were published 1974-75.

Among Ooka's 200 published books are plays and movie scripts, as well as volumes on art criticism, poetics, literary criticism, and classic poetry.

Ooka Makoto's writing has earned him a number of honors and awards. Chief among them:

1969:	Rekitei Prize for poetic theory
	(*A Family of Prodigal Sons: The Path of Modern Japanese Poetry*)
1972:	Yomiuri Prize for literary criticism
	(*Ki no Tsurayuki*)
1979:	Mugen Prize for Poetry
	(*For a Girl in Spring*)
1980:	Kikuchi Kan Prize for cross-disciplinary achievements
	(*Occasional Verses*)
1989:	Hanatsubaki Prize for Poetry
	(*Messages to the Water in my Hometown*)

Among other translations, his selected poems have appeared in English, Dutch, and French, while the linked verse on which he has collaborated has appeared in English, Dutch, and German.

Ooka Makoto was named President of the Japan PEN Club in 1989.

TAKAKO U. LENTO

Takako U. Lento writes original poetry in English and Japanese. Two of her English poems were anthologized in *A Book of Woman Poets From Antiquity to Now* (Schocken, 1980). Her published translations of Japanese poetry into English in the U.S. include a volume of the poetry of Tamura Ryuichi. She is also a co-translator of the Katydid Press volumes of the poetry of Yoshimasu Gozo and Ooka Makoto. Her translations into Japanese of Nikki Giovanni's *Gemini* and of James Baldwin and Nikki Giovanni's *A Dialogue* are published by Shobunsha (Tokyo). She has also worked with W.S. Merwin on translations of his poetry and articles into Japanese. A native of Fukuoka, Japan, she is a graduate of Tsuda College and holds a Master's degree from Kyushu University and a Master of Fine Arts in creative writing from the Writer's Workshop at the University of Iowa, where she was a Fulbright Exchange Fellow.

THOMAS V. LENTO

Thomas V. Lento has taught literature, English, and creative writing at the university level in the U.S. and Japan. A graduate of Boston College, he holds M.A. and Ph.D. degrees from the University of Iowa. He is Executive Vice President of Sardi & Bleecker, a communications agency in Princeton, New Jersey.

Asian Poetry in Translation: Japan

Editor, Thomas Fitzsimmons

Supported by the National Endowment for the Arts, the Japan-US Friendship
Commission, Oakland University (MI), University of Michigan Center for
Japanese Studies, the Saison Cultural Foundation (Japan) and UNESCO.